Digital Scrapbook Artist
User Guide

How to Contact Us

Our main office
(UK, Europe):

The Software Centre
PO Box 2000, Nottingham,
NG11 7GW, UK

Main: (0115) 914 2000

Registration (UK only): (0800) 376 1989

Sales (UK only): (0800) 376 7070

Customer Service/
Technical Support: http://www.serif.com/support

General Fax: (0115) 914 2020

North American office
(USA, Canada):

The Software Center
13 Columbia Drive, Suite 5, Amherst
NH 03031, USA

Main: (603) 889-8650

Registration: (800) 794-6876

Sales: (800) 55-SERIF or 557-3743

Customer Service/
Technical Support: http://www.serif.com/support

General Fax: (603) 889-1127

Online

Visit us on the Web at: http://www.serif.com/

International

Please contact your local distributor/dealer. For further details, please contact us at one of our phone numbers above.

Contents

Contents

Welcome

Welcome to **Digital Scrapbook Artist** from **Serif!**—the fantastic scrapbooking solution which combines scrapbooking fun with powerful drawing tools for a fantastic design experience.

Scrapbook Artist comes with **DaisyTrail DigiKits** which offer themed Content Packs, the starting point for any themed scrapbook. Each pack is full of **layouts**, **backgrounds**, **embellishments**, **materials**, **photo frames**, and decorative **letters**. Use the layouts as near ready-to-go page templates, then drag and drop items onto your page. Each Content Pack also provides supporting **effects**, **brushes**, and color **swatches** that uniquely complement the theme.

In addition to using pre-supplied scrapbook content, Scrapbook Artist also lets you **design your own** scrapbook items. Create decorative **lines**, **shapes**, and apply natural or spray brush **strokes** using easy-to-use comprehensive drawing and painting tools. Photos can be added and image corrected—you can even cut out photo foregrounds or backgrounds!

Once you've created your scrapbook masterpiece, you'll want to share it. A diverse and lively web-based scrapbooking community is available for you to share your scrapbook freely or in groups. At **www.daisytrail.com**, you're more than likely to make some new scrapbooking friends along the way too!

If you have comments or suggestions we'd like to hear from you. For complete contact information, see How to Contact Us (at the start of this User Guide).

Scrapbook features

Scrapbook essentials

- **Themes and Content Packs** (p. 11)
  Choose the type of scrapbook theme you're looking for. Themed Content Packs, such as Doll House and Enchanted, are rich in scrapbook items. Boost the number of themed Content Packs available to you from **Digikit Collections** and via **www.daisytrail.com**. Your chosen pack items are loaded in **Content tabs** ready to drag and drop onto the page—nothing could be easier!

- **Scrapbook page sizes** (p. 41)
  Design on traditional 8" x 8" or 12" x 12" pages, as well as standard Letter or A4 page formats. Or why not use a custom page size to create your own unique greetings card!

- **Cutting, erasing, and adding to items** (p. 103)
  Take your 'virtual' scissors to scrapbook material with the **Scissors Tool**—use an impressive choice of scissor cut types (Square, Pinking, Shark Fin, ZigZag, and more). Use the **Erase** and **Freeform Paint** tools to remove and add to items.

- **Design, print, and upload in high-resolution** (p. 165)
  In Scrapbook Artist, 300 dpi native working is the norm. All scrapbook items are high-resolution so quality is guaranteed. Printing and upload at 300 dpi gives truly outstanding high-quality output.

- **Layer work made easy** (see online Help)
  For greater design control, store scrapbook items on **layers**—work on items on one layer without affecting items on other layers. Layers can be created, merged, and hidden, and display a hierarchical tree view of associated items for easy selection. Apply paper textures to layer items!

● **Share via website** (p. 161)
Upload scrapbooks to Serif's scrapbook community website,
www.daisytrail.com. View layouts using powerful **zoom** technology,
give a **star rating**, **comment** on, or **search** for any scrapbook by tag.
Create public or private **groups** for like-minded scrapbookers—great
for making new friends! Take part in scrapbooking discussions in
DaisyTrail's **forums**.

Ease of use

● **Total ease of use**
Tabbed, collapsible, and dockable **Studio tabs** are always at hand.
Choose from preset colors, line styles, brushes, and effects, or create
your own. Use tabs to arrange, transform, and align items.

● **Context toolbars**
Context toolbars offer different tools and options depending on the
currently selected item. Great for efficiency and simplifying your
workflow.

● **Design aids** (p. 48)
Rotate your canvas through any angle, just like an artist would do in
real life. For more focused design, use **Solo mode** to work on an item
in isolation. Use the **Rule of Thirds** tool on your photos or on your
scrapbook page for improved page composition.

Photos

● **Adding photos** (p. 53)
Personalize your scrapbook by **importing your own photos** from hard
disk, CD/DVD, digital camera or scanner. Store photos in the **Photos
tab** before dragging directly onto a page or into a placed photo frame.

● **Photo retouching** (see online Help)
Use photo adjustments for quick fixes (or special effects) such as **Red
Eye Tool**, **Auto Levels**, **Auto Contrast**, **Brightness/Contrast**, and
many more. For advanced adjustments, applied singularly or in
combination, use the dedicated **Photo Adjustments** dialog.

- **Cropping and fitting photos to frames** (p. 70)
  Use the **Crop Tool** to remove unwanted areas of your photo. For perfect photo placement, you can **scale**, **pan**, and **rotate** photos to your liking.

- **Photo cutouts** (p. 62)
  Cutout Studio makes light work of cutting out your photos, directly within Scrapbook Artist. Use brushes to discard uniform backgrounds (sky, walls, etc.) or keep subjects of interest (people, objects, etc.).

Brushes

- **Realistic brush strokes** (p. 135)
  Unleash the painter within you with Scrapbook Artist's powerful **Brush Tool**! Apply natural or spray brush strokes using brush types from the **Brush** tab's galleries—pick brushes chosen from Content Packs, pick from preset categories, or create your own. Even apply a brush stroke around item edges!

- **Natural brush strokes**
  The **Natural Media** category hosts **Acrylic**, **Charcoal**, **Paint**, **Felt Tip**, and **Watercolor** brushes. Use **Stitching** brushes on cut materials, or why not adorn your scrapbook page with painted **ribbon**, **lace**, or **rope** effects.

- **Spray brush strokes**
  Have some painting fun with spray brushes from categories such as **Airbrush**, **Flowers**, **Fun & Celebrations**, **Glitter**, and more.

Drawing

- **QuickShapes** (p. 125)
  QuickShapes work like intelligent clipart which can morph into a myriad of different shape variations. Even extremely complex shapes like spirals, stars, and webs are simple to draw.

● **Versatile line and curve drawing** (p. 121)

For natural smooth curves, click and drag with the **Pen Tool**, even edit Bezier curve segments with selectable join options. Draw straight or freeform lines with the **Pencil Tool**. Join any line's ends to create irregular filled shapes!

● **Artistic and shape text** (p. 75)

Apply artistic text or text within QuickShapes right on the page... apply basic formatting from the always-at-hand Text context toolbar. Convert text to curves for text design freedom.

● **Color and transparency control** (p. 130)

Apply solid color or transparency to any drawn item's line or fill (or brush stroke) with the Color tab. The tab hosts color **swatches** from Content Packs, an HSL color wheel (for custom color selection), and transparency slider. Use the **Fill Tool** to apply gradient, plasma, or mesh fills for exciting results—a gradient fill path lets you add or replace colors and/or transparency simultaneously for more subtle gradients.

● **Filter effects** (p. 89)

Give your scrapbook items depth with material thickness or soft edges with feathering. Why not apply drop shadows with the **Shadow Tool** or enliven your text with fully adjustable Inner Shadow, Glow, Bevel, and Emboss filters? All are easy to apply and sure to impress.

● **Astounding 3D lighting and surface effects** (p. 96)

The Studio's **Effects tab** offers preset 3D effects (metals, elements, glass, stone, wood, and more) you can apply one or more effects, then customize by varying surface and source light properties.

Don't forget to register your new copy, using the **Registration Wizard** on the **Help** menu. That way, we can keep you informed of new developments and future upgrades!

Installation

System requirements

Minimum:

- Windows-based PC with CD drive and mouse

- Microsoft Windows® XP or Vista operating system

- 512 MB RAM

- 268 MB (recommended full install) free hard disk space

- XGA display (1024x768 resolution, 24-bit color) or higher

Additional disk resources and memory are required when editing large or complex documents.

> To enjoy the full benefit of brushes and their textures, you'll need a computer whose processor supports SSE. On brush selection, an on-screen message will indicate if your computer is non-SSE.

Optional:

- Windows-compatible printer

- TWAIN-compatible scanner and/or digital camera

- Internet account and connection required for accessing online resources and scrapbook upload

Installation procedure

1. Insert the Program CD into your DVD/CD drive.

    - If AutoPlay is enabled on the drive, this automatically starts the Setup Wizard. Follow the on-screen instructions for install.

      -or-

    - If AutoPlay is not enabled (or doesn't start the install automatically), run **setup.exe** from your CD/DVD.

2. (Optional) If you've also purchased a Scrapbook Artist DigiKit Collections DVD, install it now by inserting it into your DVD drive.

Getting started

Starting with a Content Pack theme

The Scrapbook Artist Content Packs offer a selection of themed page layouts, backgrounds, frames, materials, letters, embellishments, brushes, and effects.

If you want to get started quickly, a Content Pack theme will help you to create your first scrapbook in just a few easy steps.

You can also create original scrapbooks from scratch. (See Starting a scrapbook from scratch on p. 20.)

Additional Content Packs are available from the www.daisytrail.com website.

Choosing your theme and layout

1. Open Scrapbook Artist, or click **File>New>New from Startup Wizard...**

2. In the Startup Wizard, click **Start with a Theme**.

If you've switched the Startup Wizard off (and don't see it when you start up), you can switch it on again. Click **Tools>Options**, select the **Ease of Use** option, and then select the **Startup Wizard** check box.

3. In the **Select a Themed Content Pack** dialog, in the upper-left **Name** box, type a name for your scrapbook.

4. In the **Size** drop-down list, select a page size.

5. In the main section of the dialog, you'll see thumbnails of the installed Content Packs.

    ● Select the pack you want to use as the basis for your scrapbook.

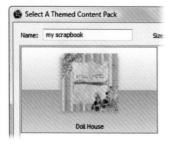

● In the **Layouts** pane, choose the pages you want to add to your scrapbook by selecting their respective check boxes.

● Click **OK**.

The first page of the layout opens in the workspace, and all of the scrapbooking items contained in the Content Pack are added to the Content tabs at the left of the workspace.

Running horizontally along the lower edge of the workspace, the **Pages** tab displays the pages you chose to add to your scrapbook.

6. Click through the thumbnails to view these pages in the workspace and choose the page you want to work on first.

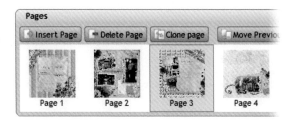

Before making any changes to the layout, let's save the file. (It's good practice to save your work frequently.)

Saving your work

The first time you save your work:

1. On the Standard toolbar, click [icon] **Save**.

2. In the **Save As** dialog:

   ● The **File name** text box displays the name you typed in the **Select a Themed Content Pack** dialog. To save your scrapbook with different file name, type it here.

   ● Browse to and select the destination for your saved file.

   ● Click **Save**.

> Scrapbook Artist periodically autosaves your work to a temporary file, allowing you to recover as much as possible in the event of a system failure. You can set autosave frequency under the **General** option of the **Tools>Options...** dialog.

On subsequent saves:

● To save the scrapbook under its current name, click the **Save** button. The existing scrapbook file is overwritten with your recent changes.

● To save the scrapbook under a different name, click **File>Save As...** to open the **Save As** dialog.

Scrapbooks are saved as files exclusively for use with Scrapbook Artist, with a *.spb file extension.

Adding your own photos

1. In the Content tabs at the left of the workspace, click the **Photos** tab to open it. At the bottom of the tab, click [Add...].

2. In the **Open** dialog, browse to and select the photos you want to add to your scrapbook.

   ● To select multiple adjacent files, press and hold down the **Shift** key, click the first file in the list, and then click the last file.

   ● To select multiple non-adjacent files, press and hold down the **Ctrl** key, and then click to select.

   ● Click **Open**. Your photos are added to the **Photos** tab.

To remove a photo from the **Photos** tab, click its ♻ **Recycle** button.

3. To replace the contents of a frame with your own photo, simply drag the photo from the **Photos** tab onto the frame (or click the **Replace Photo** button, and then browse for your new photo).

Adjusting and replacing framed photos

1. Select the photo, and then click the **Select Crop Window** button.

2. To rotate, or zoom into or out of the photo, click the buttons displayed in the lower-right corner of the photo.

3. To pan the photo, click and drag on it.

4. To close the Crop window, click Back ⬑. or click elsewhere on the page or pasteboard area.

To replace a photo:

●   Drag a different photo onto a frame from the **Photos** tab.

     - or -

●   Click the [Replace Photo] button that displays on the Photo context
     toolbar and beneath a selected photo.

Adding scrapbook letters

1.   In the Content tabs at the left of the workspace, click the **Letters** tab to
     open it.

2.   To add an individual letter, drag it from the tab onto your page.

     - or –

To add an entire word or phrase
all at once, type your text into the
box at the bottom of the tab, and
then click [Insert].

3.   You can move, resize, rotate, and delete letters individually, or you
     can work with them as a group by first clicking the [Group] button.
     (See Grouping items on p. 156.)

To work with grouped and ungrouped letters:

- To **move** an individual letter or a group of letters, simply drag it.

- To **resize** a letter or group, select it, and then drag a corner handle.

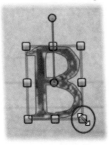

- To **rotate** a letter or group, select it, and then drag its rotate handle.

- To **delete** a letter or group, select it and press the **Delete** key.

- To **group** letters, click and drag to draw a selection marquee around them. (To avoid selecting the object beneath the letters, hold down the **Alt** key as you drag.)

  Release the mouse button and then click the Group button.

- To **ungroup**, select the group and click the Ungroup button.

Adding decorative items

1. In the Content tabs at the left of the workspace, open the **Embellishments** or the **Materials** tab.

2. Scroll the tab to find the item you want to add, and then drag it onto your page.

3. To move, resize, rotate, or delete an item, use the methods described above in Adding scrapbook letters.

Adding drop shadows

1. Select an item to which you want to add a drop shadow.

2. In the Studio tabs at the right of the workspace, click the **Effects** tab.

   In the **Preset Effects** drop-down list, the **Workspace** category contains the preset effects included in your selected Content Pack, and used in the layout.

3. Click an effect to apply it to your selected item.

Sharing your scrapbook

To share your scrapbook, you need to do the following:

1. Register on the www.daisytrail.com website.

2. Set up account information in Scrapbook Artist.

3. Upload your pages to the website.

For step-by-step instructions, see Sharing via website on p. 161.

Closing the program

To close the current scrapbook:

● On the **File** menu, click **Close**, or click the 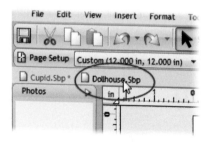 **Close** button in the upper right corner of the workspace.

- or -

If you have a middle mouse button/wheel, and multiple scrapbooks open, hover over the document's tab and click the middle mouse button.

If the scrapbook is unsaved or has unsaved changes, you'll be prompted to save it.

To close Scrapbook Artist:

● Click **File>Exit**. For each open scrapbook, you'll be prompted to save any changes made since the last save.

Starting a scrapbook from scratch

If you decide to create your scrapbook from scratch, the first step is to select your page background(s) from a Scrapbook Artist Content Pack.

Choosing page backgrounds

1. Open Scrapbook Artist, or click **File>New>New from Startup Wizard...**

2. In the Startup Wizard, click **Start with a blank page**.

> If you've switched the Startup Wizard off (and don't see it when you start up), you can switch it on again. Click **Tools>Options**, select the **Ease of Use** option, and then select the **Startup Wizard** check box.

3. In the **Content Pack Manager**, click the **Backgrounds** category.

4. In the left **Installed Content Packs** pane, select a **Content Pack** thumbnail to view its backgrounds in the **Items In Pack** pane.

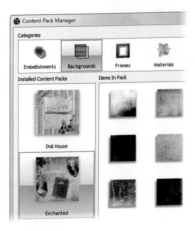

5. Click the background(s) that you want to use in your scrapbook.

   - or -

   To add all backgrounds from the Content Pack, click **Add All Items**.

   - or -

   To add all backgrounds and other items, click **Add Whole Pack**.

   The selected items are added to the **Added Items** pane.

   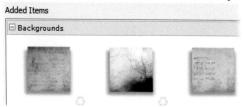

6. Click **OK**. A blank page opens in the workspace.
   In the Content tabs at the left of the workspace, the **Backgrounds** tab displays the backgrounds you added to the project.

7. Drag the background you want to use onto the blank page.

   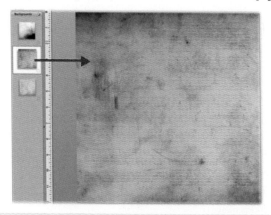

To change your background, simply drag a new background onto the page.

Before we go any further, let's save the file. (It's good practice to save your work frequently.)

Saving your work

1. On the Standard toolbar, click 🖫 **Save**. The first time you save your file, the **Save As** dialog opens.

2. Type a name for your scrapbook and then browse to and select the destination for your saved file.

3. Click **Save**.

> 📵 Scrapbooks are saved as files exclusively for use with Scrapbook Artist, with a *.spb file extension.

On subsequent saves:

- To save the scrapbook under its current name, click 🖫 **Save**.

- To save the scrapbook under a different name, click **File>Save As...** to open the **Save As** dialog.

Adding photo frames

1. In the Content tabs at the left of the workspace, click the **Frames** tab to open it.

2. If, in step 5 above, you clicked the **Add Whole Pack** button, you'll see a selection of frames in the tab.

    If you didn't choose this option:

    - At the bottom of the Frames tab, click 　Add...　.

    - In the Content Pack Manager, select a Content Pack to view its frames in the **Items in Pack** pane. (You can add frames from more than one Content Pack.)

    - Click a frame to add it to your scrapbook project, or click **Add All Items** to add them all. The items are added to the **Added Items** pane.

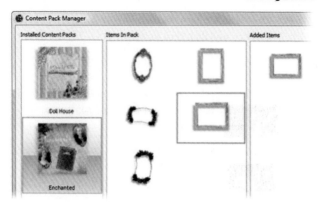

- Click **OK** to add the frames to the **Frames** tab.

3. Drag a frame from the **Frames** tab onto your page.

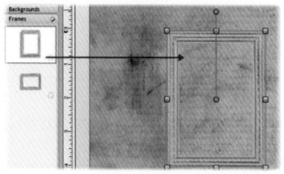

Once the frame is added to the page, you can move, resize, and rotate it. (See Arranging items on p. 149.)

Adding photos

1. In the Content tabs at the left of the workspace, click the **Photos** tab to open it. At the bottom of the tab, click Add... .

2. In the **Open** dialog, browse to and select the photos you want to add.

- To select multiple adjacent files, press and hold down the Shift key, click the first file in the list, and then click the last file.

● To select multiple non-adjacent files, press and hold down the **Ctrl** key, and then click to select.

3. Click **Open**. Your photos are added to the **Photos** tab.

▯ To remove a photo from the **Photos** tab, click its ♻ **Recycle** button.

4. Drag a photo from the **Photos** tab and drop it onto the frame, or onto the page if you don't want to frame your photo.

5. You can adjust your photo inside its frame, or replace it if required. For details, see Adjusting framed photos on p. 15 .

Adding decorative items

1. In the Content tabs at the left of the workspace, open the **Embellishments** or the **Materials** tab.

2. If you have added the whole Content Pack to your project, you'll see a selection of items in these tabs.

   If you didn't choose this option:

   ● Click **Tools>Open Content Pack Manager**.

   ● Select a Content Pack from the **Installed Content Packs** pane.

   ● In the upper **Categories** pane, click the **Materials** or **Embellishments** thumbnail to view the items associated with the selected Content Pack. (You can add items from more than one Content Pack, and from more than one category.)

   ● Click an item, and then click **Add Selected Item** (or click **Add All Items** to add them all).

   ● Click **OK**.

3. In the workspace, the items you added are displayed in the relevant Contents tab.

   To add an item to your page, drag it from its tab.

   Once an item is placed on the page, you can move, resize, and rotate it as required. (See Arranging items on p. 149.)

Adding scrapbook letters

1. In the Content tabs at the left of the workspace, click the **Letters** tab to open it.

2. If you have added the whole Content Pack to your project, you'll see the letters of the alphabet (in upper and lower case), and numbers from 0 to 9.

   If you didn't choose this option:

   - At the bottom of the tab, click Add... to open the **Content Pack Manager**.

   - In the left **Installed Content Packs** pane, select a Content Pack to view its letters in the **Items in Pack** pane.

   - Click **Add All Items** to add all of the letters (you can add individual letters if you prefer).

   - Click **OK**. The letters you added are displayed in the **Letters** tab.

3. To add an individual letter, drag it from the tab directly onto your page.

   - or -

   To add an entire word or phrase all at once, type your text into the box at the bottom of the tab, and then click Insert.

4.   You can move, resize, rotate, and delete these letters individually, or work with them as a group by first clicking the Group  button.

(See Working with grouped and ungrouped letters on p. 17, and Grouping items on p. 156.)

Applying drop shadows and other effects

1.   Select the item to which you want to add a shadow or other effect.

2.   In the Studio tabs at the right of the workspace, click the **Effects** tab.

3.   At the top of the tab, in the **Preset Effects** drop-down list, the **Workspace** category is selected by default. If you have already added effects from a Content Pack, they will be displayed in this category.

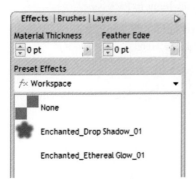

4.   (Optional) To add Content Pack effects:

●   Click **Tools>Open Content Pack Manager**.

●   Select the **Effects** category, choose a Content Pack and then click the effects you want to add to the **Effects** tab.

5.   On the **Effects** tab, click an effect to apply it to your selected item.

original   drop shadow applied

Applying transparency

You can apply transparency quickly and easily using a slider on the **Color** tab. For more advanced effects, use the **Transparency Tool** (see online Help).

To apply transparency from the Color tab:

1.   On the Standard toolbar, click ![Select] and click to select the item you want to work with.

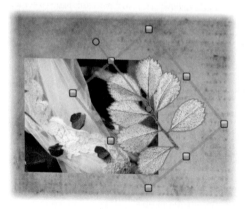

2.   On the **Color** tab, drag the Transparency slider to achieve the desired effect.

Transparency

transparency applied

Adding text

1. On the Standard toolbar, click .

2. To create text at the default size, click on your page to set a text insertion point.

    - or -

    Click and drag on your page to set the size of the text insertion point.

3. To set text attributes (font, size, etc.) before typing: Make your selections on the Text context toolbar. (See Formatting text on p. 82.)

    | A Text | Times New Roman | ▾ | 12 pt | ▾ | **B** | *I* | U |

4. To set text color, set the Line/Fill swatches on the **Color** tab. (See Changing line and fill colors on p. 130.)

5. Start typing.

> You can also create **Shape Text**, by typing directly inside a QuickShape or drawn shape. See Adding text on p. 77.

Creating brush strokes

1. On the Standard toolbar, click the  **Brush Tool**.

2. At the right of the workspace, open the **Brushes** tab. and select a brush category from the upper drop-down list.

3. On the Brush context toolbar, set the brush stroke properties (width, opacity, smoothness, etc.).

| Brush: | Colour... | Width: ↕ 32 pt ▸ | Opacity: ↕ 100% ▸ | Smoot▸ |

4. Drag a brush stroke across your page.

5. To create a new brush stroke, repeat the click and drag process.

6. When you have finished painting, to deselect the brush stroke press the **Esc** key.

Brushes used in the current scrapbook are added to the **Document** category of the **Brushes** tab.

(For more information on brushes, see Using brushes on p. 135.)

Adding Content Pack brushes

The **Brushes** tab's **Workspace** category displays the brushes added from the
Content Pack Manager. If you previously chose to add all the items from a
Content Pack, a selection of brush strokes will be displayed in this category.

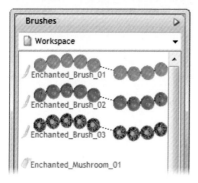

To add Content Pack brushes:

- On the Page context toolbar, click **Open Content Pack Manager**,
  choose **Brushes** from the **Categories** pane, and then click to select the
  brush(es) you want to use.

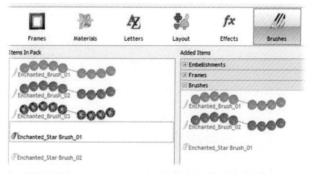

When you install a new Content Pack, the brushes included in the pack are
automatically added to the appropriate **Global** brush categories.

Arranging items and groups on the page

- To select a single item, click , and then click the item or group.

- To select multiple items, click, click the first item, then hold down the **Shift** key and click to select additional items.

  - or -

  Click in a blank area of the page, and then drag a selection marquee around the items you want to select.

- To move an item or group, select it, and then drag it.

- To resize an item or group, select it, and then drag a corner resize handle.

● To rotate an item or group, select it, and then drag its rotate handle.

● To delete an item or group, select it, and then press the **Delete** key.

See also Rotating and shearing items (p. 151), Ordering items (p. 154), and Grouping items (p. 156).

Adding pages

1. On the **Pages** tab, select the page after which you want to add your new page.

2. Click  to create a new blank page.

- or -

Click  to create a copy of the selected page.

(See also Adding and deleting pages on p. 42.)

Sharing your scrapbook

To share your scrapbook, you need to do the following:

1. Register on the www.daisytrail.com website.

2. Set up account information in Scrapbook Artist.

3. Upload your pages to the website.

For step-by-step instructions, see Sharing via website on p. 161.

Closing the program

To close the current scrapbook:

- On the **File** menu, click **Close**, or click the ⊗ **Close** button in the upper right corner of the workspace.

  - or -

  If you have a middle mouse button/wheel, and multiple scrapbooks open, hover over the document's tab and click the middle mouse button.

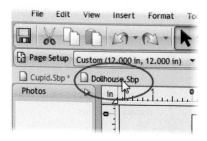

  If the scrapbook is unsaved or has unsaved changes, you'll be prompted to save it.

To close Scrapbook Artist:

- Click **File>Exit**. For each open scrapbook, you'll be prompted to save any changes made since the last save.

Opening and displaying scrapbooks

You can open an existing scrapbook from the Startup Wizard or the **File** menu. If you have more than one scrapbook open, you can switch between them using the **Window** menu or the document tabs.

Opening a scrapbook from the Startup Wizard

1.   Click the **Open Saved Work** option.

2.   In the **Open Saved Work** dialog, in the left **Documents** pane:

     ● Use the **Folders** tab to browse your computer's folder structure and locate your scrapbooks.

     - or -

     ● Use the **History** tab to view your most recently used scrapbooks.

3.   On the right, preview thumbnails of your saved scrapbooks are displayed.

     You can choose between **Thumbnails View** (displays thumbnails only), or **Details View** (displays thumbnails and information about the file—file size, creation date, and so on).

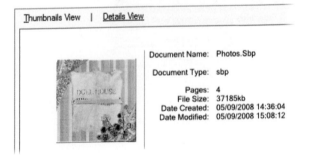

4.   Click a thumbnail, and then click **Open**.

Opening a scrapbook from the File menu

1. On the **File** menu, click **Open...**

2. In the **Open** dialog, navigate to and select the scrapbook file you want to open, and then click **Open**.

Displaying scrapbooks

If you open multiple scrapbooks at the same time, there are several ways to jump between them quickly.

Displaying a scrapbook from the Window menu:

● Select a scrapbook name from the **Window** menu.

Unsaved scrapbooks are indicated with an asterisk; the currently active scrapbook is indicated with a check mark.

Displaying a scrapbook from the document tabs:

● In the upper left area of the workspace, click on an open scrapbook's tab to make it active. The file names of scrapbooks that are not active are grayed out.

Using the Startup Wizard

Once Scrapbook Artist has been installed, you're ready to start. By default, a **Serif Scrapbook Artist** item is added to the **All Programs** submenu of the Windows **Start** menu.

Opening the Startup Wizard

- Use the Windows Start menu to open Scrapbook Artist.
  - or –
- On the **File** menu, click **New>New from Startup Wizard...**

The Startup Wizard offers different routes into the program.

Option	Allows you to...
Start with a theme	Use a Content Pack layout as the basis for your scrapbook. You can customize the layout to suit your needs by adding your own photos, text, and decorative items.
Open saved work	Open and edit saved scrapbooks.
Start with a blank page	Open a new blank page.
Tutorials	Go directly to the Scrapbook Artist "Getting Started" tutorials.

To start with a blank page, you can also click the Cancel button in the upper-right corner of the Startup Wizard.

Turning the Startup Wizard off and on

If you don't want the Startup Wizard to display every time you open Scrapbook Artist, you can turn it off at startup. (You'll be taken directly to the **Content Pack Manager** dialog instead.)

To turn off the Startup Wizard:

- In the lower-left corner of the Startup Wizard, click **Don't show this wizard again**.

- or -

1. On the **Tools** menu, click **Options...**

2. In the **Options** dialog, under **Ease of Use**, clear the **Startup Wizard** check box.

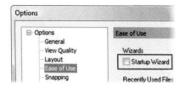

Both methods only turn the Startup Wizard off when you open Scrapbook Artist. Once the program is open, you can still access the Startup Wizard by clicking **File>New>New from Startup Wizard**.

To turn the Startup Wizard back on:

1. On the **Tools** menu, click **Options...**

2. In the **Options** dialog, under **Ease of Use**, select the **Startup Wizard** check box.
   - or -
   On the **File** menu, click **New>New from Startup Wizard**.

3. Click to clear the **Don't show this wizard again** box.

Setting up and viewing your pages

3

Choosing page size

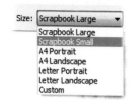

If you choose to use a scrapbook theme from the Startup Wizard (see p. 36), you can set your page size when you select your theme. Page size is set via a **Size** drop-down list in the **Select a Themed Content Pack** dialog.

Scrapbook Artist offers all the popular scrapbooking page sizes. The **Scrapbook Small** option gives you an 8" x 8" page size, which can be output to printers set up for US Letter or A4 page sizes without rescaling at time of print.

You can also create a non-standard page size by selecting the **Custom** option, and then setting your page size in the **Page Setup** dialog.

> 💡 You can change your page size at any time after you've created your scrapbook—but as a general rule, it's best to make page setup one of your first creative tasks.

> 🛑 If the Startup Wizard is turned off, or you cancel the wizard, a new blank scrapbook defaults to the custom page size (12" x 12").

Changing page size via Page Setup

1. In the Startup Wizard, click **Start with a Theme**. In the **Select a Themed content Pack** dialog, choose **Custom** from the **Size** drop-down list.

    -or-

    On the Page context toolbar, click .

2. Select a scrapbook category, by enabling a **Document Type** option button:

- For **Regular** documents, select a **Document Size**, then set the orientation (Portrait or Landscape) if using a non-square page size. For a custom size, enter a **Width** and **Height**.

- For greetings cards, select the **Special Folded** Document Type, choose **Card** or **Tent Card**. You'll see previews of each type in the **Preview** window.

3.   Adjust the scrapbook **Margins** to your specifications.

     You can set the **Left**, **Top**, **Right**, and **Bottom** margins individually, or click the **From Printer** button to derive the page margin settings from the current printer settings.

Note: Page margins are represented on the page area by solid blue guides (top, bottom, left and right). To see them, you'll need to switch guides on via **Layout Guides** on the **View** menu.

4.   Click **OK** to accept the new dimensions. The updated settings are applied to the current scrapbook.

Changing page units

The width, height, and margins of the scrapbook (its printing dimensions) are shown in **page units** (inches by default). You can change the unit without altering the scrapbook's actual dimensions.

- Choose **Options...** from the **Tools** menu and click **Layout**, then make a selection from the **Ruler Units** drop-down list.

Adding, moving, and deleting pages

A scrapbook can consist of a single page, but more typically a series of pages made up of various layouts. Pages can be added by adopting either pre-designed layouts available for Scrapbook Artist or by adding your own blank pages.

All pages are displayed in the **Pages** tab, which can be expanded from the bottom of your workspace.

Adding new pre-designed layouts

Scrapbook Artist offers a range of pre-designed Content Pack layouts on which to base your scrapbook. You can also introduce layouts into your scrapbook as new pages.

By customizing each new layout page, you can quickly create a professional looking scrapbook. See Starting with a Content Pack theme on p. 11 for more information.

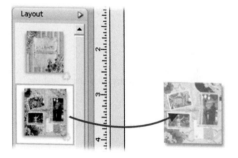

Adding blank pages

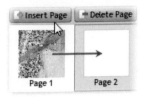

If you don't plan to work from a pre-designed layout, Scrapbook Artist lets you add blank pages from the **Pages** tab.

The new page is added after the currently selected page.

To expand the Pages tab:

● Click on the ▬▬ button at the bottom of the workspace. Click the button again to collapse the tab.

To add a new page:

1. On the **Pages** tab, select the page after which your new page will be added.

2. Click Insert Page. The new page is created and becomes the currently active page.

    -or-

    If on the last page, click the ▶ **Next Page** button on the HintLine toolbar.

Moving pages

From the **Pages** tab, you can either:

● Click and drag a page to its new position in the tab (illustrated above).

    -or-

- Select a page selected and click [Move Previous] or [Move Next]. The selected page jumps one position back or forward in the page order.

Deleting a selected page

- On the **Pages** tab, select a page and click [Delete Page] or right-click on the page and click **Delete**.

Cloning pages

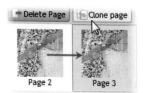

Page 2   Page 3

Use the **Clone page** button to base your new page on an existing page. Page items are copied across to the new page.

1. In the Pages tab, select the page you want to clone.

2. Click [Clone page] to create an identical copy immediately after the selected page.

Q   Reorder the pages by drag and drop if necessary.

Panning and zooming

Use panning to move around zoomed in areas of your scrapbook. To zoom, a variety of tools and magnifying options are available.

Q   If you use zooming and panning a lot, try using the Navigator tab, which is purposely designed for navigating around your scrapbook page.

Panning

Click the  **Pan Tool** on the Hintline toolbar, then use the hand cursor to click and drag anywhere on the page to reposition it in the window.

Zooming

Zoom tools on the **Hintline** toolbar allow you to view and/or edit the page at different levels of detail.

You can zoom in/out in increments, or by a user-defined or preset amount.

69% The **Current Zoom** setting on the HintLine toolbar displays the current zoom percentage, with 100% representing an actual-size page. Click over the value, to select a preset zoom from the drop-down menu (includes fit to **Full Page** or **Page Width**), or type over the value for a custom zoom percentage.

To zoom to a particular view:

- On the Hintline toolbar, click ⊖ **Zoom Out** to decrease the current zoom percentage with each click.

- Click ⊕ **Zoom In** to increase the current zoom percentage with each click.

- Click the 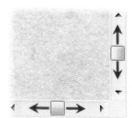 **Zoom Tool** and drag out a rectangular selection marquee on the page to define a region to zoom in to. The zoom percentage adjusts accordingly, fitting the designated region into the window. To zoom out, hold down the **Shift** key when dragging or just right-click on the page. You can also pan around a zoomed-in page while the **Ctrl** key is pressed. To zoom to the current selection, choose **Selection** from the **View** menu.

- Click the **Fit Page** button to adjust the zoom percentage so the entire page area is displayed in the window.

If you're using a wheel mouse, you can scroll the wheel forward or back to move up or down the page, or move horizontally left or right by using the **Shift** key and scrolling together. Try combining the **Ctrl** key and scrolling up or down for immediate in/out zoom control.

Navigating pages

Once you've got a page in view, you can use the scroll bars at the right and bottom of the main window to move the page and pasteboard with respect to the main window. As you drag items to the edge of the screen the scroll bars adjust automatically as the item is kept in view.

The **Pages tab** and HintLine toolbar provide a number of controls to let you navigate between pages.

Navigating with the Pages tab

Once you have added pages, use the **Pages tab** to quickly navigate between pages.

- To expand the **Pages tab**, click on the ▬▬ button at the bottom of the workspace. (Click the button again to collapse the tab.)

● To view a specific page simply select its thumbnail.

Page 3

📩 You can also use the page controls on the Hintline toolbar to navigate your pages. For details, see online Help.

Using design aids

Scrapbook Artist provides a number of tools to assist you as you design your scrapbook. Typically the tools can be switched on or off as you design.

Rotating your canvas

Rotating your canvas helps you to maintain natural flow when drawing freeform lines, curves, or brush strokes, where the artist uses the wrist as a pivot (especially when using a pen tablet). If you rotate the canvas by a chosen angle then the drawing becomes easier—taking advantage of the natural arc of the drawing hand.

The above example illustrates how grass-like brush strokes can be added to a canvas once it has been rotated 25°!

To rotate your canvas:

Either:

1. Click the 🎨⏷ **Rotate Canvas** button on the Hintline toolbar (don't click the down arrow).

2. Hover over your workspace until you see the ✋ cursor, then click and drag to rotate the canvas clockwise or counter-clockwise.

3. Once you're happy with the degree of rotation, release the mouse button to reposition the canvas.

-or-

● Click the down arrow on the 🎨⏷ **Rotate Canvas** button (Hintline toolbar) and choose a preset angle from the drop-down list.

ℹ️ You can also select an item and then choose **To Item** from the **Rotate Canvas** drop-down list. The canvas adjusts so that the item is positioned square to the X and Y axes.

To reset your canvas:

● With the button enabled, double-click anywhere on the canvas to reset

Applying the Rule of Thirds

Traditionally a technique used in photography, the **Rule of Thirds** grid can also be applied to your scrapbook to help you with page composition.

By aligning items to intersecting horizontal and vertical lines (rather than just centering items on the page) you can create scrapbooks with greater visual interest.

When a grid is applied to your page the displayed context toolbar lets you alter the grid's color and opacity. You can also add more grids, delete, and reset a grid. (See online Help.)

> The grid is actually an overlay which appears as an 'Overlay Layer' in the Layers tab.

To apply a Rule of Thirds grid:

1. Click the ⊞ **Rule of Thirds** button on the Hintline toolbar. A blue grid display over your page.

2. (Optional) Drag a corner or edge handle to resize the grid; reposition the grid by dragging. Use over selected items (instead of the entire page) depending on what you're currently working on.

3. Place embellishments, photos, or cut materials onto any of the intersecting blue lines.

Isolating an item

For focused editing, Scrapbook Artist provides **Solo mode**. This allows you to temporarily isolate an embellishment, photo, or piece of material from its page and place it on a neutral background.

- Select the item, then click 👁 **Solo Mode** button on the **Hintline** toolbar. After editing, click the button again to return to normal editing mode.

Clipping items

Clipped mode cuts off (clips) items that hang over the edge of your canvas, and which would otherwise display on your gray pasteboard area. The option is turned on by default, but you can view your overlapping items unclipped if required.

To turn off Clipped mode:

● Disable the **Clipped Mode** button on the **Hintline** toolbar. Existing and new overlapping items will then display in full. Click the button again to return to **Clipped** mode.

Working with photos

Adding your photos

You can use the following methods to add photos to your project:

- Use the **Photos** tab to store photos that you want to use in your scrapbook, then drag them onto the page as you need them.

  > Use this method if you want to add multiple photos at once, or if you want to add your photos to photo frames.

- Use the [Photo] button on the Standard toolbar to add individual images directly to the page.

  > Use this method if you want to add photos individually, or if you want to add your own embellishments to your layout.

Adding photos to the Photos tab

1. In the Contents tabs at the left of the workspace, click the **Photos** tab to open it. At the bottom of the tab, click [Add...].

2. In the **Open** dialog, browse to and select the photos you want to add to your scrapbook.

   - To select multiple adjacent files, press and hold down the **Shift** key, click the first file in the list, and then click the last file.

   - To select multiple non-adjacent files, press and hold down the **Ctrl** key, and then click to select.

3. Click **Open**. Your photos are added to the **Photos** tab.

Adding photos to the page

To add a photo from the Photos tab:

● Drag the photo from the **Photos** tab directly onto the page.

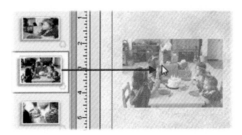

- or –

● To replace the contents of a photo frame, drag the photo onto the frame. (For more information on working with photo frames, see Adding photos to frames on p. 67.)

To add a photo from the Standard toolbar:

1. On the Standard toolbar, click .

    - or -

    On the **Insert** menu, click **Photo>From File...**

    > You can also insert photos directly from an external device such as a camera or scanner. See Importing camera and scanner images in online Help.

2. In the **Open** dialog, browse to and select the photo you want to add, and then click **Open**.

3. To insert the photo at default size, simply click the mouse.

    - or -

    To set the size of the photo, drag out a region and release the mouse button.

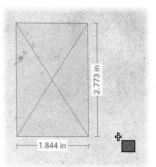

Replacing, resizing, and deleting photos

Once you've placed a photo on your page, you can replace, resize, or delete it as required.

Replacing photos

1. On the Standard toolbar, click [Select], and then click to select the photo you want to replace.

2. On the Photo context toolbar, click [Replace Photo].

3. In the **Open** dialog, browse to and select the photo you want to add, and then click **Open**.

To replace a framed photo:

● Drag a different photo onto the frame from the **Photos** tab. (See Fitting photos to frames on p. 70.)

Resizing photos

1. Select the photo with the [Select] tool.

2. To resize the photo, drag a corner handle.

The photo's aspect ratio is preserved. To allow free resizing to any aspect ratio, hold down the **Shift** key while dragging.

Deleting photos

- To remove a photo from the page, select the photo and press the **Delete** key.

- To remove a photo from the Photos tab, click its ♻ **Recycle** button.

> For information on deleting framed photos, see Deleting frames and framed photos.

Cropping your photos

Scrapbook Artist includes the **Crop Tool** for cropping objects and photos on the page. The Crop context toolbar also provides a Rule of Thirds grid to help you with your photo composition.

> For information on working with framed photos, see Fitting photos to frames on p. 70.

Cropping a photo

1. Select a photo and then on the Standard toolbar, click the ⬜ **Crop Tool**.

2.   Click and drag an edge or corner handle towards the center of the photo.

Using the Rule of Thirds

1.   Select your photo and click the **Crop Tool**.

2.   On the Crop context toolbar, click [⊞ Show/Hide Thirds Grid].

3.   A 3 x 3 grid is superimposed on top of the photo.

4.   Drag an edge handle to crop the photo. As you do so, the grid repositions itself.

5. Click and drag on the cropped photo to pan the image.

- For best results, aim to position your main subject of interest at a point where any two gridlines intersect.

- To zoom into or out of the image, use the Zoom tools.

Retouching photos

When you select a photo on the page, the Photo context toolbar displays.

In addition to replacing photos, this toolbar lets you quickly adjust brightness and contrast, remove red eye, apply auto level and auto contrast adjustments, and access a wide range of photo adjustments. For details, see online Help.

Using Cutout Studio

Scrapbook Artist includes **Cutout Studio**, a powerful integrated solution for separating objects from their backgrounds. Whether you're discarding or replacing a photo background, or isolating a section of an image to use in your layout, Cutout Studio lets you create eye-catching pictures quickly and easily.

Opening Cutout Studio

1. Select the photo you want to work with.

2. On the Photo context toolbar, click 🖌 Cutout Studio .

3. Follow the instructions outlined below.

> 💡 You'll find detailed instructions in the Help tab at the right of the Cutout Studio window.

Deciding on your approach

The approach you take depends on your photo content.

🖌 **Discard Tool:** If your subject of interest is placed against a simple, uniform background (sky, a wall, etc.), it's easier to **select and discard** the background.

🖌 **Keep Tool:** If the subject of interest is surrounded by a background consisting of complex colors or patterns (such as trees or buildings), it's easier to **select and keep** the subject.

Selecting areas to discard or keep

To select areas to discard or keep:

1.   Click the ✏ **Discard Tool** or the ✏ **Keep Tool**.

2.   On the horizontal toolbar, select a brush size.

3.   (Optional) To adjust the degree of precision with which areas are selected, select the **Grow Tolerance** check box and adjust the value.

4.   Click and drag on the image to mark the areas you want to discard/keep. As you do so, Scrapbook Artist locates similar adjoining areas and includes them in your selection.

5.   Repeat the click and drag process until your selection area is complete.

6.   As you paint your image, you can view your progress using the buttons on the left toolbar.

- 👤 **Show original:** The default view mode. The image is shown in its original form.

- 👤 **Show tinted:** Areas marked to be kept are shown with a green tint; areas to be discarded are shown with a red tint.

- 🔲 **Show transparent:** Areas marked for discarding are not shown. By default, these areas are replaced with a checkerboard background indicating transparency.

Choosing an output type

On the **Output Settings** tab, the **Output Type** drop-down list provides two output format options, **Alpha-edged bitmap**, and **Vector-cropped bitmap**. The format you choose depends on what you want to do with your resulting image.

General recommendations

Choose alpha-edged bitmap if you want to blend your cutout image into another image or background, or if your subject has poorly defined edges. Choose vector-cropped bitmap if you want to place your cutout image onto a plain or transparent background, or if your subject has more well-defined edges. (For more details on these output formats see online Help.)

To create an alpha-edged bitmap:

1. On the **Output Settings** tab, in the **Output Type** drop-down list, select **Alpha-edged Bitmap**.

2. (Optional)

   - Drag the **Width** slider to set the area of the image that is to be faded into the background.

   - Drag the **Blur** slider to smooth out the cutout edge.

3. To preview the cutout area, click **Preview**.

4. (Optional) Use the touch-up tools to further refine the cutout area (alpha-edged bitmaps only). (See Refining the cutout area on p. 65.)

5. To complete the cutout and return to the Scrapbook Artist workspace, click **OK**.

To create a vector-cropped bitmap:

1. On the **Output Settings** tab, in the **Output Type** drop-down list, select **Vector-cropped Bitmap**.

2. (Optional)

   - Drag the **Feather** slider to adjust the softening effect around the edge of the cutout. This can improve the appearance of your image.

   - Drag the **Smoothness** slider to smooth out the cutout edge.

   - Drag the **Inflate** slider to adjust the cutout outline, moving it inward or outward.

> The Inflate adjustment is particularly useful if the edges of the subject include hair or fur, which usually also incorporate some of the background color.

3. To preview the cutout area, click **Preview**.

4. To complete the cutout and return to the Scrapbook Artist workspace, click **OK**.

Refining the cutout area (alpha-edged bitmaps only)

1. On the **Output Setti**ng tab, click the **Preview** button. (You can use this button to check your cutout as you work.)

2. On the left toolbar, click the **Restore Touch-up Tool** or **Erase Touch-up Tool**.

3. Paint the areas for restoring or erasing as you would with the brush tools.

4. (Optional) To increase or decrease the opacity of the restored or erased areas, drag the **Hardness** slider (located on the horizontal toolbar).

   - Higher values will result in more pixels being erased, producing a more defined edge.

   - Lower values will produce a softer, more blended edge.

5. To complete the cutout and return to the Scrapbook Artist workspace, click **OK**.

Editing the cutout area

If you've missed a portion of the photo intended to be discarded (or just removed too much), you can redefine the cutout area at any time.

To edit a cutout:

1. Select your photo and on the Photo context toolbar, click . The existing cutout area is displayed.

2. Use the **Keep Tool** or **Discard Tool** to fine-tune your selection as described above.

Adding photos to frames

Adding photo frames to your scrapbook

Scrapbook Artist Content Packs include a wide selection of photo frames that you can add to your page. Once you've placed a frame on your page, simply drag a photo onto it—Scrapbook Artist automatically fits the photo to the frame. All frames can be moved, resized, and rotated on the page.

Adding frames to the Frames tab

1. In the Contents tabs at the left of the workspace, click the **Frames** tab to open it.

2. At the bottom of the tab, click ⌐Add...⌐ to open the **Content Pack Manager**.

    ● In the left **Installed Content Packs** pane, select a Content Pack to view its frames in the **Items in Pack** pane. (You can add frames from more than one Content Pack.)

    ● Click a frame to add it to your scrapbook project, or click **Add All Items** to add all of the frames.

    The items are added to the **Added Items** pane.

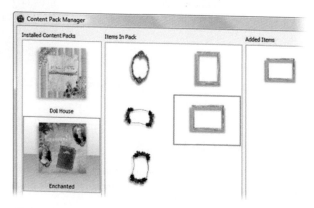

    ● Click **OK** to add the frames to the **Frames** tab.

Adding frames to the page

1. Drag a frame from the **Frames** tab onto your page.

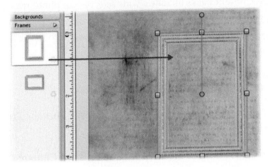

2. Once the frame is added to the page, there are various ways to work with it.

    - To resize the frame, drag a corner handle.

    - To rotate the frame, drag the Rotate handle.

3. To add a photo to a frame, drag it from the **Photos** tab. (See Fitting photos to frames.)

Fitting photos to frames

Once you have added your photos to the **Photos** tab, it's easy to frame them on the page. You can also adjust the way your photos fits inside their frames by rotating, zooming, and panning.

Adding photos to frames

1. Add your photo(s) to the **Photos** tab and some frames to the **Frames** tab.

2. Drag a photo from the **Photos** tab and drop it onto the frame. Scrapbook Artist fits the photo to the frame automatically.

Rotating, zooming, and panning

1. Select the photo, and then click the **Crop** button.

2. To rotate, or zoom into or out of the photo, click the buttons displayed in the lower-right corner of the photo.

3.   To pan the photo inside its frame, click and drag on the photo.

4.   To use the Rule of Thirds grid to help with your composition, on the
     Crop context toolbar, click [⊞ Show/Hide Thirds Grid], then click and drag
     on the photo to pan the image, positioning your main subject of
     interest at a point where any two lines intersect. (See Applying the
     Rule of Thirds on p. 49.)

5.   To close the Crop window, click [Back ⭢]. or click elsewhere on the
     page or pasteboard area.

Replacing a framed photo

●   Drag a different photo onto the frame from the **Photos** tab.

Deleting frames and framed photos

You can delete frames (along with the photos inside them) from your scrapbook
pages. You can also remove frames from the **Frames** tab.

Deleting frames from the page

● Select a frame and press the **Delete** key.

If the frame contains a photo, this will also be deleted from the page.

Removing frames from the Frames tab

● On the **Frames** tab, select a frame and click its ♻ **Recycle** button.

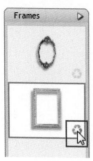

🔖 This process will only remove frames from the **Photos** tab; it will not delete frames from your scrapbook pages.

Working
with text

Working with text

You can create artistic text and shape text in Scrapbook Artist. Both text types are fully editable, and you can apply formatting, styles, and color fills before or after typing.

Text types overview

The main characteristics of artistic and shape text are outlined below.

Text type	Use and characteristics
Artistic text 	• Great for decorative typographic design. • Individual letters can be stretched, rotated, sheared, and combined with other items.
Shape text 	• Lends itself well to blocks of body text where shape and flow contribute to the overall layout. • Conforms to the containing shape. You can't manipulate individual letters, but you can achieve unique text flow effects by varying the container's properties. • Shape text does not have a line property.

Adding artistic text

1. On the Standard toolbar, click the tool.

2. To create text at the default size, click on your page to set a text insertion point.

    - or -

    Click and drag on your page to set the size of the text insertion point.

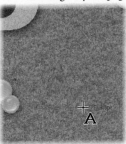

●   To set text attributes before typing, adjust the settings on the Text context toolbar. (See Formatting text on p. 82.)

●   To set text color before typing, set the **Line** and **Fill** swatches on the **Color** tab. (See Changing line and fill colors on p. 130.)

3. Start typing. To start a new line of text, press the **Enter** key.

Adding shape text

1. Create a shape from the QuickShape flyout or by closing a drawn line.

2. With the shape selected, start typing. Text flows within the shape and the **Text Tool** is automatically selected.

To set text attributes before typing, adjust the settings on the Text context toolbar. (See Formatting text on p. 82.)

To set text color before typing, set the **Line** and **Fill** swatches on the **Color** tab. (See Changing line and fill colors on p. 130.)

- To start a new line of text, press the **Enter** key.

- If you've typed more text into a shape than it can display, an
  Overflow [A] button displays below the shape when it's selected.

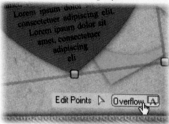

To reveal all the text:, click the [⊠] **AutoFit** button on the Text context
toolbar to reduce the size of the text, or enlarge the shape.

- To extract text from a shape (as an artistic text item), right-click the
  shape and click **Detach as New Item>Text**. To detach the text from its
  containing shape, simply drag it.

Selecting and working with text on the page

To select an entire artistic or shape text item:

- [Select] Click it with the **Select** tool.

To edit a text item:

- [A Text] Select the text item or shape, and then click the button that
  displays below the item. A text edit cursor is inserted inside the text.
  Click and drag to select the text you want to edit, and then retype. See
  Editing and deleting text on p. 81.

To move a text item:

- Select it, and then drag it.

  - or -

Click and drag its  Move button.

To resize a text item:

- Select it and drag a corner resize handle.

To rotate a text item:

- Select it and drag its Rotate handle.

To apply text formatting:

- Select the text, and then adjust the settings on the Text context toolbar. See Formatting text on p. 82.

You can also rotate and shear text items, and apply shadows, transparency, and other effects. For details, see the following sections:

- Rotating and shearing items (p. 151).

- Adding drop shadows (p. 91)

- Applying transparency (p. 98)

- Adding outlines to text (p. 85)

- Applying 2D filter effects (p. 93)

Editing and deleting text

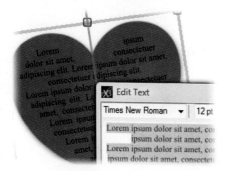

You can edit and delete artistic text and shape text on the page, or in the **Edit Text** dialog (for details on working in the **Edit Text** dialog, see online Help).

To edit text on the page:

1. Select a text item or shape with the [Select] tool.

2. Click the button that displays below the selected item, or click the [A Text] tool. A flashing text edit cursor is inserted inside the text.

3. Type new text at the insertion point, or click and drag to select the text you want to edit.

4. Type your new text.

To cut, copy, and paste text, use the standard Windows keyboard shortcuts.

To delete an entire text item:

1. Select a text item or shape with the [Select] tool.

2. Press the **Delete** key.

To delete selected characters or words:

1. Select a text item or shape with the [Select] tool.

2. Click the [A Text] tool.

    A flashing text edit cursor is inserted inside the text.

3. Click and drag to select the text you want to delete, and then press the **Delete** key.

Formatting text

You can select and format artistic text and shape text directly on the page using the Text context toolbar, the **Format** menu, or the **Edit Text** dialog.

Selecting text for formatting

To format an entire text item:

- Click the
  tool, and then click
  a text item to select
  it.

To format selected letters or words:

- Click the
  tool, and then click
  and drag to select
  one or more
  characters or words.

Using the Text context toolbar

The Text context toolbar lets you apply basic text attributes, such as point size, font style, alignment options, and so on, to selected text.

To format text from the Text context toolbar:

1. Select a text item, a character, or a group of characters.

2. On the Text context toolbar, adjust the settings described below:

- Select a text size from the **Point Size** drop-down list.

Shows the height of the selected text in points.

- Select a font from the **Fonts** drop-down list.

Lists font names and provides a preview of the selected text. Icons indicate the font type (e.g. **T** = TrueType).

- Click to apply bold, italic, or underline formatting.

- Click to apply left, center, right, or justified text alignment.

- Click to apply a bullet or numbered list style.

- Click to incrementally decrease or increase text indents.

- Click **AutoFit** to increase or decrease the size of shape text to fit its containing shape.

- Click to incrementally increase/decrease text size.

- Click to display the **Curved Text** flyout. Click a preset path to apply it to a selected artistic text item.

You can only fit artistic text to a curve.

Using the Format menu

1. Select a text item, a letter, or a group of letters.

2. On the **Format** menu, click **Character**, **Paragraph**, **Tabs**, **Bullets & Numbering**, or **Text Flow**.

3. Make your changes in the respective dialog(s), and then click **OK**.

See online Help for a detailed description of these options.

Adding outlines and edges to text

You can create interesting text effects by adding various line, brush stroke, and 'fringed' edge styles to your artistic text items.

You cannot apply lines and edges to shape text.

Adding outlines to artistic text

1. Select a text item with the 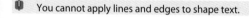 tool.

2. Open the **Line** tab.

3. To apply a line style, click one of the following buttons:

Line tab button	Effect achieved
Solid	*a*

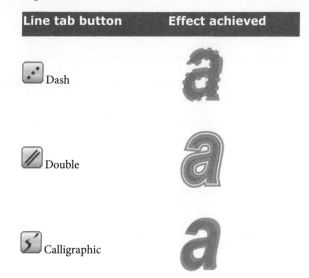

Line tab button	Effect achieved
Dash	
Double	
Calligraphic	

4.   Adjust the line width by dragging the slider.

To remove an outline, click the **None** button.

Adding brush stroke edges to artistic text

1.   Select a text item with the **Select** tool.

2.   On the **Line** tab, click the **Stroke** button.

3.   On the **Brushes** tab, select a brush stroke style.

The stroke is applied to the text outline.

4. Use the following **Line** tab controls to adjust the effect:

- Change the stroke width by dragging the slider.

- Increase or decrease the flow of the brush stroke by changing the brush **Flow** value.

Adding fringed edges to artistic text

1. Select a text item with the tool.

2. Open the **Line** tab.

3. Click the ![Edge] **Edge** button.

4. On the **Brushes** tab, select a brush stroke style.

5. Use the following **Line** tab controls to adjust the effect:

- To apply the edge style *inside* the edge of the text, select the **Inner Edge** check box.

- Change the stroke width by dragging the slider.

- Increase or decrease the flow of the brush stroke by changing the **Flow** value.

Applying
effects

7

Adding drop shadows

Each Content Pack comes complete with ready-to-go drop shadow effects. These are selectable, and available at the same time as you select embellishments, backgrounds, layouts, etc.

Once you've chosen your effect, you can select it from the Effects tab's **Workspace** gallery. When applied, the selected item adopts the drop shadow effect (see rightmost moon).

If you want more effect control, the ▢ **Shadow Tool** is great for allowing freeform control of the drop shadow effect. With its on-the-page control nodes and supporting Shadow context toolbar, the tool offers various adjustments such as Opacity, Blur, and X (or Y) Shear.

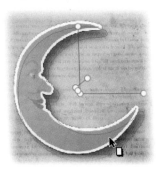

Simple shadow
(drag from item center)

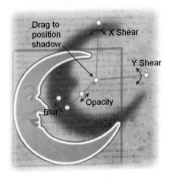

Offset shadow

(showing control nodes)

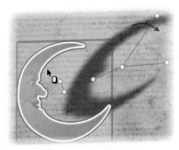

Skewed offset shadow

(adjusted X Shear)

> Once you've created a basic shadow, you can further edit it as needed using the Filter Effects dialog.

Applying drop shadows with Shadow Tool

1. Click the ▢ **Shadow Tool** on the **Standard** toolbar. You'll notice control nodes appear which allow adjustment as described in the annotated illustration above.

2. Drag across the item to create a drop shadow (note additional nodes being created).

3. Change blur, opacity, or shear accordingly with nodes (or via the displayed context toolbar).

To change a shadow's color:

● Select the item, choose the **Shadow Tool**, and then select a color from the Studio's **Color** tab.

To remove the shadow from an item:

● Double-click the item while the **Shadow Tool** is selected.

Applying other 2D filter effects

Changing material thickness

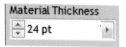

If you've been manipulating materials you've added to the page, perhaps by cutting out with the **Scissors Tool,** you can apply some depth to your material by applying an embossing effect.

● From the **Effects** tab, adjust the **Material Thickness** setting on your selected item. The greater the value, the greater the embossed effect.

Making feathered edges

Feathering applies a softer edge to your scrapbook items, such as embellishments or cut materials. The effect is especially useful for presenting a photo on the scrapbook page.

● From the **Effects** tab, pick a **Feather Edge** setting.

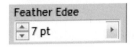

This is the distance inside the item's outline from which feathering will be applied.

In the **Filter Effects** dialog, the **Feathering** option offers independent control of **Opacity** and **Blur**, which can also be used in conjunction with other 2D filter effects.

Applying filter effects

For more advanced control of filter effects, Scrapbook Artist provides a variety of **filter effects** that you can use to transform any item. The following examples show each filter effect when applied to the letter "A."

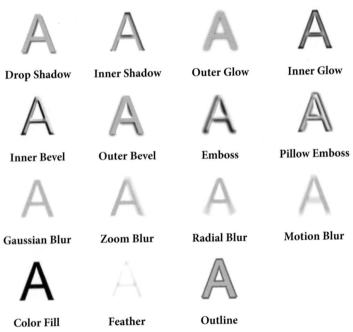

Drop Shadow	Inner Shadow	Outer Glow	Inner Glow
Inner Bevel	Outer Bevel	Emboss	Pillow Emboss
Gaussian Blur	Zoom Blur	Radial Blur	Motion Blur
Color Fill	Feather	Outline	

Scrapbook Artist additionally provides the **Shadow Tool** for applying a shadow to an item directly on your scrapbook page. Control handles let you adjust shadow blur, opacity and color.

To apply 2D filter effects:

1. Select **Filter Effects...** from the **Format** menu (or via the right-click menu). The **Filter Effects** dialog appears.

2. To apply a particular effect, check its box in the list at left.

3. To adjust the properties of a specific effect, select its name and vary the dialog controls. Adjust the sliders or enter specific values to vary the combined effect. (You can also select a slider and use the keyboard arrows.) Options differ from one effect to another.

4. Click **OK** to apply the effect or **Cancel** to abandon changes.

Creating outlines

Scrapbook Artist lets you create a colored outline around items, especially text and shapes (as a **filter effect**). For any outline, you can set the outline width, color fill, transparency, and blend mode. The outline can also take a gradient fill, a unique **contour** fill (fill runs from the inner to outer edge of the outline width), or pattern fill and can also sit inside, outside, or be centered on the item edge.

As with all effects you can switch the outline effect on and off. You'll be able to apply a combination of 2D or 3D filter effects along with your outline, by checking other options in the Filter Effects dialog.

Blur

Various blur effects can be applied to Scrapbook Artist items. The types of blur include:

- **Gaussian**: the effect smoothes by averaging pixels using a weighted curve.

- **Zoom**: applies converging streaks to the image to simulate a zoom lens.

- **Radial**: applies concentric streaks to the item to simulate a rotating camera or subject.

- **Motion**: applies straight streaks to the item to simulate the effect of camera or subject movement.

Applying 3D filter effects

As well as 2D filter effects, Scrapbook Artist provides a variety of **3D filter effects** that you can use to transform any item. Such effects are selectable from an Effects tab which offers an impressive choice of ready-to-go simulated natural and man-made surfaces. When applied to drawn items, previously "flat" appearances are brought to life by application of depth and texture.

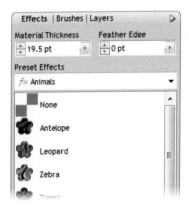

The **Effects** tab displays a variety of thumbnail presets in various categories (Glass, Metal, Animals, etc.).

Click any thumbnail to apply it to the selected item.

 None of these 3D effects will "do" anything to an unfilled item—you'll need to have a fill there to see the difference they make!

Customizing 3D filter effects

Once an effect has been applied, you can customize it via the **Filter Effects** dialog.

1.   Select the item with a 3D effect applied.

2.   Select **Filter Effects...** from the **Format** menu.

3.   In the **Filter Effects** dialog, you'll notice the **3D Effects** and **3D Lighting** boxes already be checked.

4.   Experiment with the effect by checking various sub categories (e.g., 3D
     Bump Map, 2D Bump Map, etc.) and adjusting the options on each
     pane.

Paper textures

Paper textures simulate textures of varying roughness and "feel" by selection of
various real media textures such as **Canvas**, **Cartridge**, **Embossed**, **Parchment**,
and **Watercolor.** As a paper texture is a layer property the same layer's texture
will be applied to all items on that layer. A different texture can only be applied
to a different layer (and to all its items).

Applying paper textures

1.   In the **Layers** tab, decide on which layer you wish to apply a paper
     texture.

2.   Click the ▨ **Paper Texture** button shown after that chosen layer's
     name and, from the dialog, select the **Paper Textures** category. A
     gallery of texture thumbnails is displayed.

3.   Choose one of the thumbnails and adjust percentage **Scale** and
     Opacity if needed.

4.   Click **OK**. The button will change to indicate that a paper texture has
     been applied, e.g. ▨. Existing or any subsequently new items will
     adopt the paper texture once applied.

Removing a paper texture

1. Click the **Paper Texture** button on the layer from which you want to remove a paper texture.

2. From the dialog, simply click the **Remove** button. The paper texture is removed from all items on the layer.

You can also swap or remove paper textures from within the **Layer Properties** dialog (right-click on a layer entry and choose **Layer Properties...**).

Applying transparency

Transparency effects are great for highlights, shading and shadows, and simulating "rendered" realism. They can make the critical difference between flat-looking illustrations and images with depth and snap.

Transparency may seem a bit tricky because by definition, you can't "see" it the way you can see a color fill applied to an item. In fact, it's there all the time in Scrapbook Artist. Each new item has a transparency property: the default just happens to be "None"—that is, no transparency (opaque).

Transparencies work rather like fills that use "disappearing ink" instead of color. The more transparency in a particular spot, the more "disappearing" takes place there, and the more the item(s) underneath will show through.

Solid
(100% opaque)

Gradient
(100% to 0%
opaque)

Solid
(50% opaque)

Solid transparency distributes the transparency equally across the item. **Gradient** transparencies are created by drawing a path across the item; Linear transparencies are drawn by default but other categories such as **Radial**, **Ellipse**, **Conical**, **Plasma**, **Square**, **Three Points**, and **Four Points** can be created.

Applying solid transparency

The **Color** tab hosts a **Transparency** slider, which controls the level of **solid** transparency applied to currently selected items.

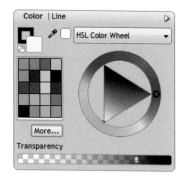

The further right the slider, the more opacity; the further left the more transparency. Remember that opacity is the inverse of transparency—100% Opacity = 0% Transparency, and vice versa.

To apply solid transparency with Color tab:

1. With your item selected, open the **Color** tab.

2. Adjust the **Transparency** slider to set the level of transparency. The transparency is applied to the item(s) uniformly.

Applying gradient transparency

Just as a gradient fill can vary from light to dark, transparency can be applied as a opacity gradient, by drawing a gradient transparency path across the item (e.g., from 100% opacity to 0% opacity).

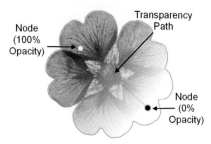

Node (100% Opacity)

Transparency Path

Node (0% Opacity)

For items with gradient transparencies (Linear, Radial, Ellipse, etc.) you can adjust the transparency effect by adding or subtracting nodes along the gradient transparency path. The **Transparency Tool** can display an item's gradient transparency, indicated by two or more nodes situated along a path. You can reposition the nodes to adjust the transparency's starting point or end point, or if more than two nodes are present, intermediate levels of transparency along the path.

For transparencies with multiple nodes, each node has its own value, comparable to a key color in a gradient fill. Each selected node's value can be altered directly on the page or by using the **Gradient Transparency Editor** dialog.

To apply gradient transparency with Transparency Tool:

1. Select an item.

2. Click the  **Transparency Tool** on the **Standard** toolbar.

3. Click and drag across the item to define the transparency path. The item takes a simple Linear transparency, grading from 100% opacity to 0% opacity. The effect starts where you place the start node, and ends where you place the end node.

Changing transparency type

Solid ▼
Solid
Linear
Radial
Conical
Ellipse
Square
Three Points
Four Points
Plasma
Bitmap

By default, the **Transparency Tool** will let you apply only a linear transparency on the drawn path. However, the tool's context toolbar lets you change to one of several transparencies, e.g. Radial, Conical, Ellipse, Plasma, etc.

The path's appearance may change to reflect the transparency type but the principles of editing the transparency path are the same.

Editing gradient transparency

Once you've applied a gradient transparency, you can adjust its **path** on the item, and the **level** of transparency along the path. You can even create more complex transparency effects by adding extra nodes to the path and assigning different values to each node.

Each node along the path is selectable by clicking and can therefore adopt its own transparency value.

To adjust the transparency path:

1. Select the item with a gradient transparency.

2. Click the ![Transparency Tool icon] **Transparency Tool** on the **Standard** toolbar.

3. Drag the displayed nodes to new positions. You'll notice the effect change as you drag a node.

Editing a **gradient transparency** path is similar to editing a comparable fill path. Adding a level of transparency means varying the transparency gradient by introducing a new **node** and assigning it a particular value. For transparencies with multiple nodes, each node has its own value, comparable to a key color in a gradient fill.

You can either edit the path directly using the **Transparency Tool** in conjunction with the **Color** tab, or use the **Gradient Transparency Editor** dialog exclusively (this is similar to the **Gradient Fill Editor**). Both methods let you define key values along the path.

The dialog lets you fine-tune the actual spread of transparency between pairs of key values, and displays the transparency gradient, with pointers marking the nodes (corresponding to nodes on the path) that define specific transparency values. Again, black represents 100% opacity, and white represents 0% opacity, with grayscale values in between. A sample window at the lower right shows the overall transparency effect.

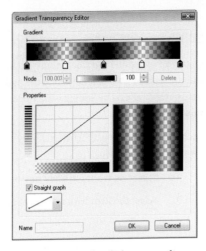

For details of how to edit and manage transparency via this dialog, see online Help.

Cutting, cropping, and erasing

Cutting and splitting items

Use the **Scissors** tool to cut any item or group of items on your page. For example, you might want to cut a material or embellishment, or add a decorative cut edge to a photograph.

You can cut freeform shapes, or apply a preset cutter shape.

Cutting freeform shapes

1. Use the **Select** tool to select one or more items.

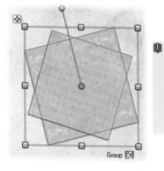

> To cut through selected items on multiple layers, ensure that the **Edit All Layers** button, on the **Layers** tab, is selected.
>
> (See Working with layers in online Help.)

2. On the **Standard** toolbar, click the **Scissors Tool**.

3. On the Scissors context toolbar, select a scissor type from the drop-down list.

4. Optional:

    ● To adjust the regularity of the freeform cutting line, adjust the
      Smoothness setting.

      To do this, click the up and down arrows, or click the right arrow
      and drag the slider.

    ● To adjust the length of each unit of the cutting edge, change the
      Wavelength setting.

• To adjust the depth of each unit of the cutting edge, change the **Amplitude** setting. (You can't adjust wavelength or amplitude for **Straight** cutting lines.)

5. To create a freeform cut, click and drag across the item(s).

Unselected items that the cutting line crosses will not be split.

6. To remove a cut section, click it.

- or -

To retain a cut section, hold down the **Shift** key, and then click the section you want to retain. (All other portions of the item will be deleted.)

- or -

To retain both sections and split them apart:

- Click the 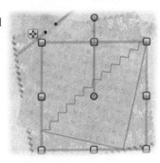 tool and then click a cut section.

- Drag the section into its new position.

Applying preset cutter shapes

1. Use the 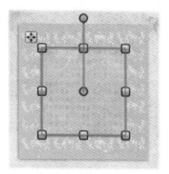 tool to select one or more items.

2. On the Standard toolbar, click the  **Scissors Tool**.

3. On the Scissors context toolbar, select a scissor type from the drop-down list.

～～～ Pinking	▼
———— Straight	▲
⊓⊔⊓⊔ Square	
～～～ Wavy	
～～～ Pinking	
⋏⋏⋏⋏ Double ZigZag	
⋌⋎⋌⋎ Triple ZigZag	
⌒⋏⋏ Diagonal	
⋏⋏⋏ Saw	
⋏⋏⋏ Spike	
⌒⌒⌒ Fence	
⌣⌣⌣ Spacer	

4. Click to expand the **Preset Scissor Paths** flyout, choose a shape and then click to apply that cutout shape to your item.

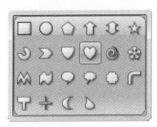

5. The preset shape is applied to the item. Click the **Cut** button in the lower-right corner.

6. To delete or retain cut sections:

    ● To delete a cut section, click it.

    ● To retain a cut section, hold down the **Shift** key, and then click the section.

-    To retain both sections and split them apart, click the **Select** tool, then click a cut section and drag it into its new position.

Combining, cropping, and joining items

Scrapbook Artist provides the powerful **Combine**, **Crop**, and **Join** tools (**Add**, **Subtract**, and **Intersect**), which you can use on multiple selections to create new shapes.

You can access these commands from the **Arrange** tab, the **Arrange** menu, or from the menu accessed by right-clicking on a multiple selection.

Arrange tab buttons

 Combine
Merges selected items into a
composite item, with a hole
where filled regions overlap.
The composite takes the line
and fill of the bottom item.

Click the button again to break the item apart.

 Crop and Clip flyout

Crop to Top
The bottom item is
cropped to the outline of
the top item.

Crop to Bottom
The top item is cropped to
the outline of the bottom
item.

Clip to Top
The bottom item is clipped
to the outline of the top
item.

Clip to Bottom
The top item is clipped to
the outline of the bottom
item.

Crop and **Clip** create a temporary composite item.

(To break the item apart later, click **Arrange>Crop>Uncrop**.)

 Join/Add
Creates a new item that's the sum of two or more selected items, whether or not they overlap.

 **Join/Subtract**
Retains only the portion of the bottom item that is not overlapped.

(Useful for cutting out shapes from photos.)

 Join/Intersect
Retains the overlap and discards the rest.

Add, **Subtract**, and **Intersect** produce a permanent new item out of any selected items. You can only break the resulting item apart *immediately* after creating it by clicking the **Undo** button on the **Standard** toolbar.

Erasing and adding to items

Erasing   **Adding to**

Scrapbook Artist provides the following tools for erasing and adding to existing lines and shapes.

Erase

Lets you erase portions of a selected item or items. You can control the extent of erasing by setting eraser tip width and pressure (if using a graphics tablet).

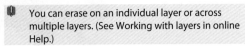

You can erase on an individual layer or across multiple layers. (See Working with layers in online Help.)

Freeform Paint

Lets you add to or 'grow' the boundary of an existing shape or line. This tool is especially useful for reshaping existing items, or for creating unusual filled shapes.

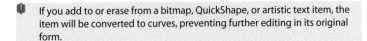

If you add to or erase from a bitmap, QuickShape, or artistic text item, the item will be converted to curves, preventing further editing in its original form.

Erasing portions of an item

1. Use the  tool to select an item.

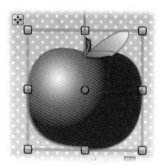

2. On the **Standard** toolbar, click the ⬜ **Erase Tool**.

3. On the context toolbar, choose an eraser tip shape.

Tip: ◯ ▢ ◇

4. (Optional) Set the tip width by adjusting the **Width** value.

5. Position the ◖ cursor, and drag over the item's edge. The area to be erased is drawn temporarily (use the **Ctrl** key to redefine the erase area while drawing).

6.   Release the mouse button to erase the area drawn.

Adding to an item

1.   Use the 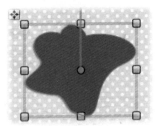 tool to select an item.

2.   On the **Standard** toolbar, click the  **Freeform Paint Tool**.

3.   On the context toolbar, choose a shape for the tool's tip.

Tip: ○ □ ◇

4.   (Optional):

● Set the tip width by adjusting the **Width** value.

● To create a series of shapes without switching tools, click to disable the ☐ Select-on-Create button.

5.   Position the  cursor over the item and drag over an item boundary.

You'll see blue shading, which represents the area to be added.

6.   Release the mouse button to reshape the item to include the painted area.

Adding lines
and shapes

Drawing lines and shapes

Lines can be either straight or curved. They have properties like **color** and **weight** (thickness). When a line (or series of line segments) forms a complete, enclosed outline, it becomes a new **closed** item called a **shape**. Because shapes have an interior region that can be filled with a solid color or gradient fill, they have **fill properties** as well as **line properties**. QuickShapes, ready-to-go shapes in Scrapbook Artist, take a line and fill color too.

As soon as you draw a line you'll see the line's **points** appear. The line between any two points is called a line segment. Freeform and curved lines usually have many points; straight lines have only two.

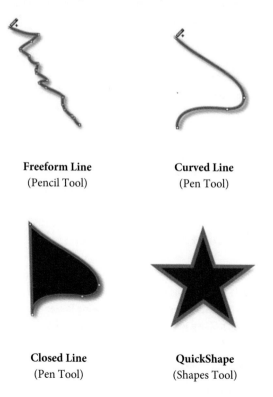

Freeform Line
(Pencil Tool)

Curved Line
(Pen Tool)

Closed Line
(Pen Tool)

QuickShape
(Shapes Tool)

Drawing freeform lines

1. Choose the ![pencil icon] **Pencil Tool** from the **Standard** toolbar.

2. Click once, then drag across the page, drawing a line as you go. The line appears immediately and follows your mouse movements.

3. To end the line, release the mouse button. The line will automatically smooth out using a minimal number of points. Note the dots indicating its points—at the two ends, and at each point where two line segments come together.

4. (Optional) To set the degree of smoothing to be applied to the line (and subsequent lines), set the **Smoothness** value (by entering a value or adjusting the slider) on the context toolbar.

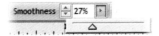

🎤 To draw a straight line, hold down the **Shift** key down as you drag.

Drawing curved lines

Curved lines are created as a series of connected line segments (which may be curved or straight) using a series of "connect the dots" mouse clicks. New line segments are added all the time. The tool is designed for drawing complex, combination curves and shapes in a highly controlled way.

1. Choose the ![pen icon] **Pen Tool** from the **Standard** toolbar.

2. ![curve icons] From the displayed context toolbar, choose to create your drawn segments in **Smooth joins** or **Sharp joins** creation mode. By default, you'll be in **Smooth joins** mode (i.e., drawing Bézier curves segment-by-segment). Sharp joins would create a zig-zag line without curving through points.

3. Click where you want the line to start (**1**).

4. Click again for a new point and drag out a pair of **control handle** which orbit the point (**2**). (Control handles act like "magnets," pulling

the curve into shape. The distance between handles determines the depth of the resulting curved line.)

5. Release the mouse button to create your curve segment (**3**).

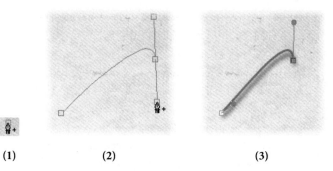

     (**1**)   (**2**)   (**3**)

6. To extend an existing line, click beyond the end of your current curve to create a new point (thus creating another curve segment). Normally, curve segments end in a symmetric (evenly rounded) corner (**4**), with control handles locked together.

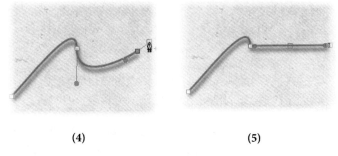

          (**4**)   (**5**)

7. However, you can press the **Alt** key while drawing the segment to define a "cusp" or sharp corner (**5**). This locks the control handle on the last created point. For more on line corners, see Editing lines and shapes.

8. To end the line, press **Esc** or choose a different tool.

Drawing shapes

To close a freeform line or curve as you draw:

- For irregular shape, simply extend the line back to its starting point. Shapes have an interior which is filled with the current **default fill** (see Changing line and fill colors on p. 130) when the line or curve is closed.

To close an existing line or curve (with a straight line):

1. Select the line or curve with the **Select** button (**Standard** toolbar).

2. Click the Edit Points button under the item.

3. Select **Close Curve** button from the context toolbar. A straight segment appears, closing the curve.

If you're trying to draw a cartoon outline made up of many independent curves (e.g., a cartoon ear, rose, etc.) you may want to fill each curve without closing it. This is made easy by using the **Fill-on-Create** feature.

To fill an unclosed curve automatically:

- Select the **Pencil Tool**, **Pen Tool**, or **Brush Tool** (**Standard** toolbar).

- Enable the **Fill-on-Create** button from the context toolbar, and select a suitable fill from the **Color** tab. You'll also need to ensure **Select-on-Create** is enabled on the context toolbar.

- Draw a freeform line into a curve. The resulting curve is closed automatically and filled with the current fill color.

Drawing QuickShapes

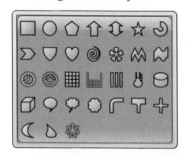

QuickShapes are pre-designed items that you can instantly add to your page. QuickShapes are added from a flyout containing a wide variety of commonly used shapes, including boxes, arrows, hearts, spirals and other useful symbols.

Once you've drawn your QuickShape, you can adjust its properties—for example, apply solid fills, gradient fills, or apply transparency effects. You can even use sliding **control handles** to create variations on the original QuickShape.

It's also possible to use the QuickShape context toolbar situated above the workspace to swap QuickShapes, and adjust a QuickShape's line weight, color, style, and more.

To create a QuickShape:

1. Click [Shapes] on the **Standard** toolbar and select a shape from the flyout.

2. At your chosen cursor position, either:

   ● Double-click to place a default-sized QuickShape.

   -or-

   ● Click and drag on the page to draw out your QuickShape to a chosen size. To constrain the aspect ratio (for example, to obtain a square or circle), hold down the **Shift** key while dragging.

3. New QuickShapes adopt the currently set line and fill in Scrapbook Artist.

   All QuickShapes can be positioned, resized, rotated, and filled. What's more, you can adjust their designs as soon as they are drawn, or at a later time.

For example, you can:

- Drag the handles on a Quick Polygon to make a triangle, pentagon, hexagon, or other polygon.

- Drag the handles on a Quick Box to make corners more or less rounded.

- Drag the handles of a Quick Oval to change the oval into a "pie" shape.

To adjust the appearance of a QuickShape:

1. Select the item with the ▶ Select button (**Standard** toolbar).

2. Click the Edit Points ▷ button under the item. This reveals sliding round handles around the shape. Different QuickShapes have different handles.

3. Drag the handle to change the appearance of a QuickShape.

    For example, dragging the top sliding handle to the right on the QuickStar below will produce a very different star shape.

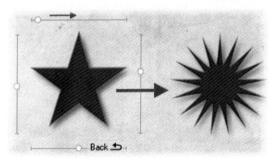

Changing line style

All lines, including those that enclose shapes, have numerous properties, including color, style, line ends, weight, join (corner), and cap (end).

Using the Studio's **Line** tab, you can adjust **plain line** properties for any freeform, straight, or curved line, as well as for the outline of a shape.

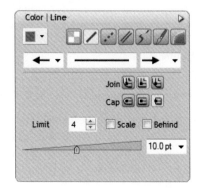

Changing line color

 The color swatches selected from your themed Content Pack become available under the **Line** tab's **Color** drop-down menu. You can still apply custom colors via the **More Colors...** option on the drop-down menu, or simply work from the **Color** tab.

For more details on adding or editing plain line colors, see Changing line and fill colors on p. 130.

Changing line style

A series of buttons arranged along the top of the tab set the line style. **Solid**, **Dash**, **Double**, **Calligraphic**, and **Stroke** styles can be used. A fringed **Edge** style can be applied to shapes and text. Each style applies a very different look to your line.

To change line style:

● Simply click a button to set the line style—only one style can be set any one time. Pick another button to jump to that style.

Once a style is selected you can choose line ends for most styles (except **Stroke** and **Edge**). For some styles, various variations are also available. For example, for a **Dash** or **Double** line style, various additional dash patterns (below) and double line options can be selected.

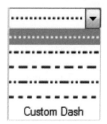

To select a line end:

● From the ⬅️▾ and ➡️▾ drop-down menus, pick a line start and end.

Two styles called **Stroke** and **Edge** let you apply a brush, chosen from the **Brushes** tab, to your line or your shape's edge. You'll see your current brush shown in the **Line** tab. Both styles look great when applied to artistic text.

Other styles such as **Dash** and **Calligraphic** offer further customization of the chosen style.

Changing line caps and joins

The **Line** tab also lets you vary a line's **Cap** (end) and the **Join** (corner) where two lines intersect. Both properties tend to be more conspicuous on thicker lines; joins are more apparent with more acute angles. The respective button icons clearly communicate each setting:

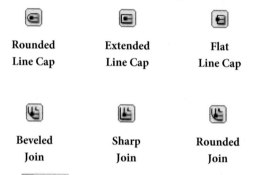

Rounded Line Cap	**Extended Line Cap**	**Flat Line Cap**

Beveled Join	**Sharp Join**	**Rounded Join**

The ☑ Behind check box controls line width relative to item size—useful with very small items or when resizing text. When checked, the inner half of the item's line appears behind its fill; otherwise, the whole line appears in front of the line.

Check the ☑ Scale check box to automatically expand and contract the line thickness in proportion to the item size (or uncheck to make the line's thickness remain unchanged). When scaling text, for example, you might either want the border to remain the same width, or change in proportion to the overall characters.

Changing line width

On a selected line, curve, or shape (opposite), drag the **Weight** slider in the **Line** tab. To turn off the line, set the box to 0.0pt.

Changing line and fill colors

For complementary design, you can select swatch colors as well as your scrapbook items when you've chosen your Content Pack. A category called **Swatches** lets you include a range or colors ideal for use with the chosen Content Pack. Once selected via the Content Pack Manager, these colors become available in the **Color** tab's **Workspace** palette, which shows by default.

Any closed shape, such as a closed curve or QuickShape, or text has an interior region that can be filled. The fill type can be solid, gradient, or plasma. Those that use a single color are solid fills.

The **Line/Fill** swatches on the **Color** tab govern whether the selected color is applied as a line color or a solid fill.

To use a Workspace palette's color for the line or fill, you can click on any of the tab's color swatches.

To use a non-palette color instead, choose a color from the **Color** tab's HSL Color Wheel.

You can swap to a different palette within the Palette Switcher by clicking the `More...` button. A comprehensive series of pre-supplied color palettes are available, either RGB or CMYK standard palettes or one of a range of themed palettes (e.g., Soft Tones).

Changing line color

1. Select the item, a freeform line or curve.

2. Set the **Line/Fill** swatch in the **Color** tab so the **Line** swatch is active, then pick a color from the palette or HSL Color Wheel.

Changing fill color

1. Select the shape.

2. Set the **Line/Fill** swatch in the **Color** tab so the **Fill swatch** is active, then pick a color from the palette or HSL Color Wheel..

Applying tinted colors

A **Tinting** option in the **Color** tab's drop-down menu allows a percentage of shade/tint to be applied to your color.

1. With the **Line/Fill** swatch set accordingly (for line or fill; see above), select **Tinting** from the **Color** tab's **Color Mode** drop-down menu.

2. Drag the slider to the right to add white to the starting color (for a lightening effect), or drag left to add black for a darkening effect. You can also enter a percentage value in the box (0% resets to the original color).

Applying transparent fills

● Click ▢ **No Fill** on the **Color** tab's **Line/Fill** swatch, which represents either None (a transparent interior for items with line/fill properties) or Original (for pictures only, to reset the item to its original colors). See Applying transparency on p. 98.

Applying gradient fills

Gradient fills are those that use gradients—small "spectrums" with colors spreading between at least two defined **key** values. Specifically, gradient fills include the **Linear, Radial, Ellipse, Conical, Square, Three Color,** and **Four Color** types.

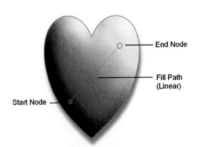

Once you've drawn your line or shape you can use the **Fill Tool** to draw a fill path across the item, and then edit the item's **fill path**.

1. Select the item.

2. Click the [icon] **Fill Tool** on the **Standard** toolbar.

3. Click and drag on the item to define the fill path (a solid line). The item takes a simple **Linear** fill, grading from the current color of the item, ending in white (items filled with white will grade from white to black, to show contrast).

To change the fill type:

- From the Fill context toolbar, choose a fill type from the drop-down list.

The item displays a fill path which differs according to which fill has been chosen. The path can then be edited.

Editing gradient paths

1. Select an item with a gradient fill.

2. Click the ![Fill Tool] **Fill Tool** button on the **Standard** toolbar. The item's fill path appears.

3. Use the **Fill Tool** to drag the start and end circular path nodes, or drag on (or outside) the item for a new start node, creating a new fill path as you drag. The gradient starts where you place the start node, and ends where you place the end node.

4. To constrain the fill path in 15° increments, hold down the **Shift** key while dragging. On Ellipse fills, **Ctrl**-constraining also forces the gradient's aspect ratio to match the item's bounding box.

Each gradient fill type has a characteristic path. For example, Radial fills have single-line paths, with the gradient initially starting at the item's center. Ellipse fills likewise begin at the center, but their paths have two lines so you can adjust the fill's extent in two directions away from the center. Radial fills are always evenly circular, while Ellipse fills can be skewed in one direction or another.

Editing the path means adjusting the path's node positions and/or adding, deleting, or changing key colors on the path. Nodes are added by clicking on the path, and are selectable to allow for their deletion and for key colors to be altered.

To edit an item's fill color(s) and tint:

1. Select a node on the fill path, then choose a different **Fill Start** and **Fill End** from the context toolbar. Alternatively, pick a color/tint from the Color tab's palette or color wheel.

-or-

2. Right-click the selected item and choose **Format>Fill...** (or choose the command from the Format menu). Use the **Fill Editor** dialog to add/remove nodes, modify node colors and alter node positions along the path. See Editing gradient fill spectrums or Working with plasma fills in online Help.

Specific adjustment techniques and **Fill Tool** options differ for each of the basic fill categories.

Using brushes

Adding brush strokes

 Add artistic flair to your scrapbooks with the **Brush Tool.**

The **Brushes** tab galleries include both  natural stroke and spray brush types (see Choosing brush types on p. 138).

Select from a wide range of preset categories, or add themed Content Pack brushes to your workspace. If you're feeling really creative, you can even create your own custom brushes. (For information on creating and customizing brushes, see online Help.)

You can draw and paint with your mouse or with a pen tablet. The tablet's pressure-sensitive pen tip allows control of stroke width or transparency (see Pressure sensitivity in online Help).

Choosing brush types

Brush types

Scrapbook Artist brushes are categorized as follows:

- **Airbrushes**
  Add dramatic, soft, or textured airbrush effects.

- **Edges**
  Apply inner or outer edge effects to any shape.

- **Flowers**
  Paint your pages with flower and leaf spray brushes.

- **Fun & Celebrations**
  Create cheerful, fun layouts with confetti, sweets, stardust, and clouds.

- **Glitter**
  Make your pages sparkle with glitter dust and glitter glue brushes.

- **Grunge**
  Add aged and grunge effects to your layouts.

- **Natural Media**
  Apply paint, charcoal, pencil, pen, and other natural media brush strokes.

- **Photo**
  Add realistic lace, rope, ribbon, and rope effects with this collection of photo brushes.

- **Stitches – Collection**
  'Stitch' items to your page with these colorful brushes.

- **Stitches – Eyelets**
  Use these brushes to add interesting eyelet stitch effects.

Selecting brushes from the Brushes tab

The **Brushes** tab lets you view brushes currently being used in your scrapbook, and serves as a container for supplied brush presets, themed Content Pack brushes, and your own brush designs.

Document category

The **Document** category shows the brush types used in the currently active scrapbook.

This category is useful for 'bookmarking' brushes for easy reuse.

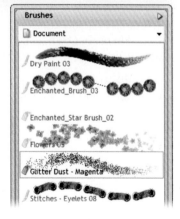

Global category

The **Global** category stores the supplied brush presets under a series of pre-defined subcategories.

You can add, rename and reorder any category and even create nested categories within categories.

These brushes are available to all scrapbooks currently open.

> When you install a new Content Pack, the brushes included in the pack are automatically added to the appropriate **Global** brush categories.

Workspace category

The **Workspace** category displays the themed brushes added from the Content Pack Manager.

See Adding brushes from Content Packs, below.

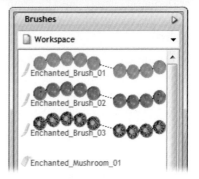

Adding brushes from Content Packs

1. On the Page context toolbar, click **Open Content Pack Manager** (or click **Tools>Content Pack Manager**).

2. In the **Content Pack Manager**, select a **Content Pack** from the left pane.

3.   In the upper **Categories** pane, click **Brushes**.

4.   The **Items in Pack** pane displays the themed brushes contained in the selected pack.

     Click to select the brush(es) you want to use.

     - or -

     To add all brushes from the pack, click **Add All Items**.
     The brushes are added to the **Added Items** pane.

     (To remove a brush from this pane, click its ♻ Recycle button.)

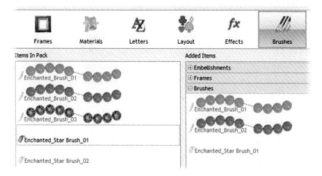

5.   Repeat steps 2 to 4 to add more brushes, if required (you can add brushes from multiple Content Packs).

6.   To add the brushes to your workspace, click **OK**.

7.   On the **Brushes** tab, the Content Pack brushes are displayed in the **Workspace** category.

If you're creating your own brushes you can create your own brush categories by right-clicking on the tab's **Category** drop-down menu. (See online Help.)

Creating brush strokes

You can apply brush strokes directly to the page using your mouse or pen tablet. If you're using a pen tablet, you can control stroke width and transparency by adjusting pressure sensitivity (see Pressure sensitivity in online Help).

Applying brush strokes

1. On the **Standard** toolbar, click the **Brush Tool**.

   The Brush cursor indicates that the **Brush Tool** is selected and that you're ready to paint.

2. On the **Brushes** tab, choose a brush from a category.

    At the top of the workspace, notice that the Brush context toolbar is
    displayed. Use this control to set the properties of your brush stroke.

The following steps provide an overview of the brush properties. For more details,
see Setting brush stroke properties on p. 144.

3. Click the **Color** button and select a brush stroke color using the **Color
    Selector** dialog. (You can't change the stroke color of the brushes in
    the **Workspace** category of the **Brushes** tab.)

4. Set the **Width, Opacity**, and **Smoothness** for your brush stroke.

    To change, click the up and down
    arrows, or clicking the right arrow
    and then dragging the slider (as
    shown for smoothness opposite).

5. (Optional) If you want to fill your closed or unclosed shape as you
    paint (see illustration below):

    Enable the
     button,
    and then set the Fill color
    swatch on the **Color** tab.

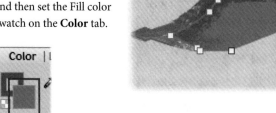

6. (Optional) If you want to be able to edit your strokes immediately
    after painting them, enable the ⬚ Select-on-Create button.

7. With the brush cursor drag a brush stroke across your page.

🔲 The properties currently defined on the Brush context toolbar settings will be adopted for all brush strokes.

After this first brush stroke, there are two ways in which you can paint subsequently, depending on whether you have enabled the **Select-on-Create** option.

• **Edit, then paint**

If **Select-on-Create** is not enabled, when you release the mouse button, the stroke you just created is not selected. If you want to edit or add to the stroke, you must first select it.

🔲 Use this method when you're happy to set all your brush stroke properties *before* painting—and particularly if you intend to paint repeatedly with the same brush stroke style.

• **Paint and edit**

If **Select-on-Create** is enabled, when you release the mouse button, the stroke you just created is automatically selected, allowing you to add to or edit it immediately.

🔲 Use this method when you want to change your brush stroke properties (color, width, opacity, etc.) frequently.

🔲 Press the **Esc** key to deselect the current brush stroke.

A brush stroke can be extended or reshaped, as for a straight or curved line (see Editing lines and shapes in online Help). The brush stroke path can also be reversed, closed, or opened.

Setting brush stroke properties

You can set the properties of your brush strokes (both before and after creating them) using the Brush context toolbar.

To set the brush properties of a brush stroke:

1. To set properties before painting, click the 🖌 **Brush Tool** and choose a brush style from the **Brushes** tab.

To set properties of an existing brush stroke, select the stroke.

The Brush context toolbar displays.

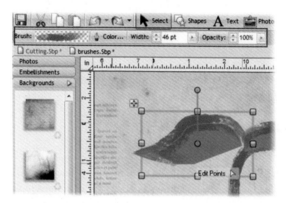

2. Change the brush design by selecting from any category on the
   Brushes tab.

3. Click the **Color...** button to change the brush stroke color using the
   Color Selector dialog.

   - or -

   Set the line swatch on the **Color** tab.

   (See Changing line and fill colors on p. 130.)

   Brush strokes cannot take a gradient fill. If applied, the base color of the fill is
   adopted.

4. Adjust the brush stroke **Width** setting by entering a value, clicking the
   up/down arrows, or clicking the right arrow and then dragging the
   slider.

   -or-

Set the brush stroke width on the **Line** tab. (You can also set brush stroke color on the **Line** tab.)

5.   Adjust the **Opacity** of the brush stroke. (100% opacity = no transparency; 0% opacity = fully transparent.)

-or-

On the **Color** tab, drag the **Transparency** slider to achieve the desired effect.

6.   If, in step 1, you selected the **Brush Tool** rather than an existing brush stroke, you'll see three additional options on the context toolbar: **Smoothness**, **Select on Create**, and **Fill-on-Create**.

●   To set the degree of smoothing to be applied to the brush stroke, set the **Smoothness** value (by entering a value, clicking the up/down arrows, or dragging the slider).

●   ☐ Select-on-Create   Click to enable or disable this option.

Select-on-Create disabled: When you release the mouse button, the stroke you just created is not selected. If you want to edit or add to the stroke, you must first select it.	💡 Use this method when you're happy to set all your brush stroke properties before painting—and particularly if you intend to paint repeatedly with the same brush stroke style.
Select-on-Create enabled: When you release the mouse button, the curve or stroke you just created is automatically selected, allowing you to add to or edit it immediately.	💡 Use this method when you want to change your brush stroke properties (color, width, opacity, etc.) frequently.
	🔌 Press the **Esc** key to deselect the current brush stroke.

Fill-on-Create Enable this option if you want to fill the unclosed curve produced with a brush stroke with the fill color defined on the **Color** tab. (See Changing line and fill colors on p. 130)

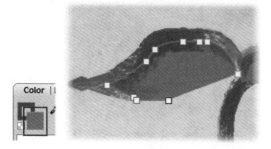

Arranging
items

Rotating and shearing items

Rotating items

1.   Select the item(s) with the  tool.

2.   Hover over the rotate handle and, when you see the cursor change, drag in the direction in which you want to rotate the item.

As you drag, the angle of rotation is temporarily displayed around the item's origin point (shown as ⊙). This temporary display of information is known as **tool feedback**.

- To rotate in 15° intervals, press and hold down the **Shift** key while dragging.

- To revert the rotation, double-click the rotate handle.

To change the rotation origin point:

1.   Click and drag the origin point to any position on the page. (This can be outside the item itself—useful for rotating grouped items around a central point.)

2. Drag the repositioned rotate handle. The item rotates about the new origin point.

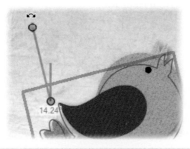

Additional rotation options are provided on the **Arrange** and **Transform** tabs, and on the **Arrange** menu. For details, see online Help.

Shearing items

1. Select the item(s) with the **Select** tool.

2. Hover over a centre edge handle. When you see the Shear cursor, click and drag in the direction in which you want to shear the item, and then release.

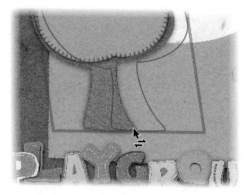

- To copy and shear an item, press and hold down the **Ctrl** key while dragging—this preserves the original item, while shearing the new copied item as you drag.

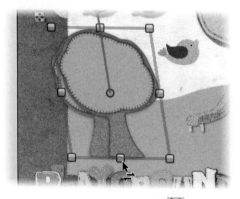

- For precise shearing, enter an exact **Shear** value in the Transform tab.

Ordering items

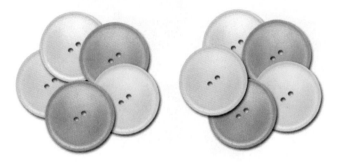

The items on your scrapbook page are 'stacked' on top of each other, the front-most item (e.g., blue button above) being the one on top of the stack (also known as **Z-order**).

Each time you create a new item, it is placed in front of the items already there. You can move any item to any position in the ordering sequence using buttons on the Arrange tab below. The yellow button in the first illustration above has been moved to the front.

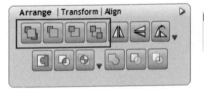

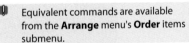
Equivalent commands are available from the **Arrange** menu's **Order** items submenu.

To change an item's position:

On the **Arrange** tab, click one of the following buttons:

-  **Bring to Front**

-  Send to Back

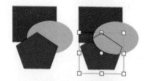

- Back One

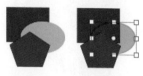

- Forward One

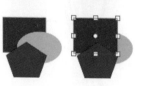

Don't confuse the concept of item ordering with that of page layers. (See Working with layers in online Help.)

Grouping items

Grouping items prevents you from accidentally altering them.

Grouping also allows you to move, rotate, and resize items all together, and to edit similar items all at the same time.

You can select multiple items at the same time but this is a temporary operation; grouped objects are always kept together until you physically ungroup them. The only requirement for grouping is that multiple items are selected in advance (see p. 31).

To create a group from a multiple selection:

● Click the Group button below the selection.

To ungroup (turn a group back into a multiple selection):

● Click the Ungroup button below the selection.

In general, any operation you carry out on a group affects each member of the group. For example, property changes applied to a group—such as changing line or fill—will affect all the items contained in the group.

You can select and edit items within groups, without having to ungroup them.

To select an individual item within a group:

● Press and hold down the **Ctrl** key and then click on the item. The item is selected and can be edited.

● To deselect the item and its group, click elsewhere on the page.

Sharing and publishing

12

Sharing via website

You can share your scrapbook by print, as a distributable electronic PDF, or via the **www.daisytrail.com** website. Publishing your scrapbook to website means you can share your scrapbook not just with friends and family, but with a community of like-minded scrapbookers!

The **www.daisytrail.com** website is designed specifically as a scrapbook community. By uploading your completed scrapbook to the website, just like other Scrapbook Artist users do, you add to the collection of published scrapbooks in the community.

The main website features include:

- **View published scrapbooks**
  To aid scrapbook design or to browse for fun, use the **Wall** scrapbook gallery which "showcases" public scrapbooks published by other Scrapbook Artist users (... and yourself!). Take advantage of awesome **zoom** technology coupled with pan and zoom control. Easily view your own, the most recently uploaded, and most popular scrapbooks.

- **Scrapbook rating**
  Rate and comment on other people's scrapbooks—and have your own scrapbook assessed by the community. Award five stars to the very best!

- **Work in groups**
  Create groups of users with similar interests—great for schools, clubs, or maybe just your network of scrapbooking friends. Use the **Group Wall** to view published scrapbooks in a chosen group, which can be private, public or "friends only." Post to **group forums** restricted to just group members.

- **Search**
  Find scrapbooks, groups, or other scrapbookers throughout the website.

- **Make new friends!**
  Social networking meets scrapbooking! Use **email** or user discussion **forums** to build friendships with other scrapbookers, especially those you add to your friends list. Even upload photos of yourself!

- **Profile management**
  Manage your tagline, password, time zone, language, and email notifications.

To share, three stages need to be carried out—register on the website, setup account information in Scrapbook Artist, and then upload your chosen scrapbook to the website.

Registering

1. Click [⇧ Share] on the **Standard** toolbar.

2. If you've not registered before, click the **Join Now!** button. You'll be taken directly to **www.daisytrail.com** registration.

3. From the registration form, enter your personal information, including an email address to which an activation message will be sent. Use the **Help** button if needed.

4. Click **Create Account**. For account activation, you'll need to check your email and click on the activation message sent to you. This may take time depending on your ISP and connection!

Remember your Username and Password! You'll need to re-enter this information into Scrapbook Artist.

5. Registration is complete after activation. All that's now required is to enter your account details into your Scrapbook Artist program.

6. If you've already registered but not added your account details, click **Login**. This takes you to your account details where you can enter details as described in the next section.

So you don't forget to set your Daisytrail user account details, you'll get a reminder to register every eight days if there are no details set. You can register on the website, then transfer your username and password over, or cancel to register later.

Setting up account details in Scrapbook Artist

1. Select **Options...** on the **Tools** menu.

2. In the **Upload** pane, enter your **Username** and **Password**.

3. (Optional) click the [Test] button to verify that the account details are correct. If successful, a "*Username and password valid*" message is produced.

   If you've forgotten your password or you've not already registered, use the accompanying **Reset Password** and **Register** buttons. For the latter, you'll be directed to the Registration page on the website. Complete the registration details and click **Create Account**.

4. (Optional) Reduce the upload **Quality** to 96 dpi to speed up file transfer if your Internet connection is 56k dial-up modem (at the expense of zoom quality). Otherwise, use the default 300 dpi for broadband and all other faster Internet connections.

If you change your account details on the website at a later date, you'll also need to make these account changes in Scrapbook Artist.

Uploading

Once you've successfully created your account you can upload your scrapbook, with the option of including only specific or all pages.

☑ Page 1   ☑ Page 2   ☐ Page 3

To upload your scrapbook:

1. On the **Standard** toolbar, click .

2. In the **Share** dialog, uncheck pages you don't want to upload (use the scroll bar to view all pages).

3. (Optional) For the upload you can choose a different account to upload to. Enter a different **Username** and **Password**.

4. Click ⟨ Upload ⟩ to transfer your selected pages.

5. On upload, a progress bar indicates upload status. On completion, click **OK** to close the dialog or click **View** to immediately see your uploaded scrapbook on the website.

Basic printing

Scrapbook Artist supports printing directly to a physical printer (e.g., All-in-ones, Inkjet and Laser printers), with options for scaling and thumbnail printing.

To print:

1. Choose **Print...** from the **File** menu, or after right-clicking on the page or pasteboard.

2. From the **Print** dialog, select the number of pages to print, and optionally a print size (as original, scaled, or as thumbnails).

3. Click the **Print** button.

Exporting as PDF

The cross-platform **Adobe PDF** file format is a worldwide standard for document distribution which works equally well for electronic or paper publishing. It excels as an electronic distribution medium as it is device- and platform-independent.

To make scrapbook sharing easy, Scrapbook Artist lets you export your scrapbook as a PDF file (Acrobat 4.0 compatible). In doing so, all your scrapbook's colors will be output in an RGB color space, and all scrapbook pages will be rasterized (converted to bitmaps) on export.

Exporting as a PDF file

1. Choose **Export as PDF...** from the **File** menu's **Export** submenu.

2. From the dialog, select a **Print Range**:

    - **Entire Scrapbook**: exports the whole scrapbook.

    - **Current page**: exports only the page currently displayed.

    - **Pages**: enter a page range (e.g., 3-5) to export a limited selection of pages (or individual page numbers, if separated by commas). If you've set a range, you can further export just odd or even pages in the range from the drop-down list.

3. (Optional) Set various options as follows:

    - For more convenient on-screen viewing in Adobe Reader, you can check **Fit to complete page** or **Fit to page width** to specify how the scrapbook will initially appear.

    - Check **Optimize for Fast Web View** to insert code that allows PDF streaming if your file is downloaded for viewing in a Web browser. This feature provides pages "on demand" for rapid visibility—so for example if the reader switches to page 9, page 9 will download next. Bear in mind that you'll see a distinct benefit from PDF streaming only if your file is to be opened from a Website. Enabling the feature will add to the time it takes to publish your file.

    - Uncheck **Preview PDF file** to stop your PDF file from displaying in your currently installed Adobe Reader immediately after exporting. If checked, you'll get your file displayed immediately after export finishes.

4. (Optional) Select a **Print Quality** level from the drop-down list. **Best** quality offers 300 dpi lossless export (no compression). Other list options offer lower resolution export, with smaller file sizes offered as quality decreases.

5. Click **OK** to proceed to export.

6. From the dialog, choose a location and file name for your PDF file. Click the **Save** button.

    Once export completes, the PDF displays if **Preview PDF file** is checked.

Index

Index

Index